Crossing Barriers:
Sharing Food and North Korean Escape Memories

Helen Hahn-Steichen

DEDICATION

This book is dedicated to my mother and grandmother and to all mothers who love their families courageously.

ACKNOWLEDGMENTS

I gratefully thank my mom and my dear friends, Donna Vander Griend, Sheela Word, Lisa Fritzke, Sister Kathy Riley, Annie Liwag and Sharon Robnett for their valuable input on different drafts of this book:

Special thanks to my Fanstory friends especially: Patti Sanchez, Heidi Mitchell, Marla Thurman, Yvonne Uzzell, cumulus365, Pharp, doggymad and Turtlestage5

Additionally, I am grateful to Venise Lee who provided five of the photographs used here.

Last but not least, this book couldn't have been completed without the love, support and technical help from my husband.

Dear Reader:

I am Korean American and I grew up hearing the Korean accent all my life. It wasn't until I took a phonology class during a master's program that I learned to really appreciate how a person's first language influences the pronunciation of a second language. I found the way sounds are replaced unconsciously fascinating. So I have come to value the various accents I heard in my life.

In this story, one of the characters, Eunhae, has a strong Korean accent and I wanted to convey that to you. In Korean, there are no "f," "th," "v," or "z" sounds. So unconsciously, she substitutes sounds: f as p; th as t or d; v as b; and z as j. It is surprising how often an "s" in written English is actually a "z" sound when spoken.

Although Korean has distinct "r" and "l" sounds, "r" occurs at the beginning of syllables and "l" at the end, so sometimes "r" and "l" sounds are confused. Also, when an "s" sound is followed by a long "ee" sound, the "s" becomes a "sh" sound. Thus, the word, "calcium" would be pronounced as "calshium."

Portraying this incomplete picture of an accent adds a word puzzle to your reading. But by slowing you down, I wanted you to have the experience of hearing her voice just as Lisa and Maddie had to put extra effort in listening for comprehension. I try to retain most of the regular English spelling to avoid more confusion.

Thank you for your patience in reading.

Helen Hahn-Steichen

1 A New Neighbor

I strained to listen for sounds down the hall, as morning lightened the shade of gray on my bedroom window. The welcome silence encouraged me to sneak out to enjoy a quiet breakfast. Feasting on a toasted plain bagel with a weak cup of tea in silence had become a rare luxury lately.

Suddenly, I spied a gossamer thread out of the corner of my eye. Spiders are busy in the fall, so I worked quickly to grasp it but I realized it was my own fine hair, now more silver than blonde. In annoyance, I corralled my hair into a ponytail, a hairdo I avoided in public as it accentuated my large, long nose and my wide-set eyes. With a ponytail, I have the unfortunate resemblance to a bird, a hen perhaps.

I picked up my latest detective novel and read as I ate. I started where I last left off when my concentration was constantly punctured by my chatterbox roommate.

> *"The private investigator calmly confirmed that the victim was killed simply with a poisonous white powder sprinkled on the donuts."*

My stomach tensed as I feared poison most of all the ways to die.

A sudden staccato knock produced chills and prickles on my arms. I tiptoed toward the door.

At first, no one was visible through the peephole. I looked down and saw the dark hair of a small lady holding a plate full of round things covered *in white powder*. Since she didn't have a clipboard and pen, nor a wad of pamphlets, I felt safe enough to open the door in spite of the mysterious white powder. Perhaps she was my new neighbor across the street.

Neighbors just are neighbors. They live nearby so you just think you will always have that chance to get to know them. But how *do* you get to know them? Some people greet a new neighbor by bringing a plant or a plate of cookies to welcome them.

Once, I had a Japanese neighbor, whose tradition dictated that new residents must introduce themselves to the others by bearing gifts. The young couple went down the entire block of thirteen houses to greet each neighbor with a small gift. Most were not home. Some were vaguely polite and accepted the gift like one would accept a brochure and closed the door. But when they came to my door, I invited them in for tea. I don't know why. I imagined how hard it was to be a stranger in a strange country. That first meeting led to more meetings and memories of a good friend.

So I opened the door to greet a new Asian neighbor. Although she was short, she looked very solidly built. She held a small plate full of circular dessert-looking things covered *in a white powder*. They were not big enough to be cupcakes but more substantial looking than cookies. It was enough to spark my curiosity but not my appetite.

"Hi. I'm Eunhae... My name eej Eunhae and I ribe dere," she said, pointing to the house across the street.

"Oh. Hi! I'm Lisa. Good to meet you," I responded just like a dialogue straight out of an English language textbook.

"Risa?"

"Yes, LLLisa," I replied overemphasizing the initial 'l' sound.

I guessed that this wasn't going to be an easy conversation. But as I could see she was doing her best to be friendly, I motioned to invite her in. She responded with a violent windshield wiper motion in front of her face. I didn't learn until later that I needed to make the offer several more times to assure her that this was a genuine offer. She handed me the plate of unknown goodies.

"Today is Chuseok so I wanted to share dis wid you," she said like a child who had faithfully practiced a line for the school play and was finally able to deliver it.

"Uh. Choo-what? Oh, thank you. They're so pretty," I said, hesitating as I hated to try new foods especially those covered by an unknown white powder.

"Chuseok ij holiday in Korea. Big get-togeder like Tanksgibing holiday here. All de pamily get togeder. Important day to me aj my grandpader got out ob .... Pree prom..." she said as she grasped both hands on some invisible bars and banged on some invisible walls.

"Um ... jail? Prison?" I guessed as I was very good at charades.

She nodded vigorously. "prom jail."

"What? Why was he in jail?"

"Becauje he run away prom Nort Korea." She placed her forefinger on her chin and searched the sky for some figure. "Dis in nineteen porty seben," she added.

"1947?"

More vigorous nodding followed. Then she abruptly smiled, waved goodbye and left me holding the curious dessert things. I was even more bewildered about the partial story she told me.

"Ooooh! Mochi!" cried Maddie, my roommate. "I love mochi. Where did you get them?" It was as if she smelled the scentless delicacies from down the hall or there was some irresistible magnetic pull.

"My - I mean - *our* new neighbor across the street..."

"You're sharing right?" Maddie asked as she reached for one of the round things and shoved the whole thing into her mouth.

"MMMMM!" she hummed as she closed her eyes enjoying the flavors.

Suddenly, her eyes bulged open and one hand reached for her throat and the other held her upper chest. Maddie raced to the kitchen and coughed violently into the sink. I followed behind, placed the plate on the counter to free my hands, just in case I might need to use my rusty first aid training.

Maddie calmly got a glass of water and immediately gulped down half of it. Then she took a deep breath and exhaled. She turned to the plate and took another piece.

"What are you doing? You're crazy! You nearly died just now."

"Nah, I ate too fast. The rice dough is too chewy for speed eating."

"Speed eating? Is that a new sport?" I replied incredulously. "By the way, what is that stuff anyway?"

"It's mochi. It's a Japanese dessert made of sweet rice flour filled with sweet bean paste. I think it's adjukbns," she said as she took another bite.

"What?"

"Adzuki beans. Small red beans. See?" At this point, Maddie whipped out her cellphone from her back pants pocket with her right hand while her left hand kept feeding her mouth. She was careful to avoid getting the white powder on her phone screen. With a quick tap dance of her right thumb, she brought up pictures of the bean. This was one of her super powers, being able to think of a topic and bring it up on her cellphone screen a second later.

"And what's the white powder?" I asked.

"Oh, that's just cornstarch."

Maddie came to live with me in an emergency situation. Her brief marriage was in a state of separation and she needed a place to stay until she could earn enough for her own place. I resisted as I love my quiet, monastic existence but a mutual friend from church insisted we give it a try. That friend had an ominous twinkle in her eye as she said, "You'd be so good for each other."

After briefly skimming her phone screen about the little red beans, I saw with horror that all the mochi were gone.

"You ate them all?"

"No, I saved one for you," Maddie said guiltily putting the one in her hand back onto the plate.

"No, it's okay. I don't do well with beans, anyway."

"No! You have to try one. At least, taste it."

Maddie pulled out a knife from the silverware drawer and divided the last piece in half.

"Here. Try half. Besides, what are you going to say if she asks you how you liked it?"

"That's easy. I'll say my roommate enjoyed them all before mmmph." I couldn't finish as a soft, squishy half a mochi was being shoved in my mouth. It was as if I was given a whole pack of bubblegum to chew all at once. The rice part was mostly bland and chewy but the beans were just like a chocolate substitute, like carobs.

"And it's so smart, you know because combining beans and rice is getting a full complement of proteins. So it's healthy!"

"I'm not so sure about the sugar though…" I managed to say after successfully swallowing.

"So this neighbor is Japanese?"

"No, she's Korean."

"Yeah. Right. Korean cuisine has those mochi cakes, too but they call it something else. You can ask her when you return her plate."

"But that means I have to make something, too."

"Why?"

"Remember my Japanese neighbor? She taught me that when someone brings you something in a container, you must never return it empty."

Maddie snapped her fingers and said, "Got it! Here's what we'll do…"

"We?" My eyebrows shot up in alarm. And so began another kitchen adventure with "Internet Maddie." Despite fearing the apocalyptic effect on the kitchen this could have, I was anxious to return the plate and ask about the North Korean escape. History books paint events in broad, general strokes but learning about real people living through those events makes them come alive.

2 Snakes in a Dream

"Tada!" Maddie exclaimed after she artfully arranged about
a half dozen peanut butter cookies on Eunhae's plate.
"Now we can return the plate full! And I'm so glad you
agreed to use the recipe with only peanut butter, eggs and
sugar."

"Okay," I said as I pulled out the last cookie sheet from
the oven. "Can you put some plastic wrap over it?"

"Whaaat?" Maddie replied accusingly. "What if the plastic
melts on the warm cookies? Plastic is very bad for your
health! How about foil instead?"

"Aluminum?" I countered. "Isn't that bad for your health, too?"

"How about wax paper then?"

"Okay."

Then as we walked out the door, we had more squabbles.

"You don't need to lock the door!" Maddie complained. "We're just going across the street."

"Yeah, but we don't know how long we'll be there."

"Who's going to come in and steal your books?"

I just sighed and locked the door and pocketed my keys. Life with a roommate has certainly challenged every one of my daily activities. For the past three months, my reclusive life was invaded by the presence of another human being and what a noisy human she was. Maddie either talked or sang incessantly. Even when alone in her room with the door shut, there were noises from her internet shows and video games. Silence was rare.

Maddie practically skipped across the street and rang the doorbell. Ten seconds passed. I rang it again.

Eunhae opened the door with wide-eyed surprise at our unannounced arrival. But she quickly recovered and her face brightened into a welcoming smile.

"Hi Risa! Good to shee you!" she said and looking with admiration at Maddie, she added, "Ij dis your daughter?" Oh, how I hated that question. Why, when Maddie was only ten years younger, did everyone assume she's my daughter? And why can't a single middle-aged woman be happily husbandless and not have children or grandchildren? I must have looked flustered as Maddie jumped right in.

"Hi, I'm Maddie. I'm her roommate...at least for now."

"Oh, nice to meet you," Eunhae smiled and nodded at Maddie. Her accent was not so noticeable when she used her most practiced phrases.

"Come in, come in!" she said and pulled Maddie in by the hand. My hands were occupied by her plate with our cookies so I had no idea how strong she was but Maddie looked a bit startled.

"Oh, it smells wonderful in here!" Maddie gushed.

I crossed the threshold a bit more warily and the pungent smell of garlic, onions and ginger assaulted my nose.

"Sorry, I was just making kimchi," she confessed with some embarrassment.

"I love kimchi!" Maddie was really ecstatic now. I was going to see if she had a mute button on her but seeing that her statement gave Eunhae some delight, I backed off.

"Dats great! No worry. I gibe some to you!" Eunhae said marveling at Maddie's appreciation of Korean cuisine.

Eunhae motioned us to sit at her small, round dining table. I looked around and saw that everything was unusually tidy and like my house, had no indication of a male inhabitant.

Eunhae got tea water boiling and brought several yellow apples and a cutting board to the table. Before we could object, she was slicing and peeling apples in an unusual way. Some slices had strips of skin left on like a cape. Other slices were partially peeled and were stacked to resemble a swan.

"Pleaje eat." Eunhae said as she placed the plate of decoratively sliced apples in front of us.

"Why do you peel the apples?" asked Maddie as she examined the slices. "The skin is full of vitamins."

"Yes, but ip pretty, you enjoy look and enjoy plabor more."

"And you eat it slowly to enjoy and digest it better, right?" I said giving Maddie a sideways look.

"Right," agreed Eunhae.

"Where did you learn to cut fruit like that?" I asked as Maddie reached for her third slice.

"Ebery girl needj to do dis. In Korea, dey say ip a girl cannot cut like dis, she cannot get hujband."

Maddie visibly bristled at this piece of information and asked, "So what does a boy have to learn to get a wife?"

Eunhae put the knife down and laughed hysterically. Neither Maddie nor I thought it was that funny.

Thinking this would be a good time to change the subject I interjected, "By the way, you mentioned about your grandfather? I was curious about how he escaped from North Korea."

"Oh, dat. Yes, my grandmoder tried to rescue him so she went back to Nort Korea to look por him."

"Whaaat?" Maddie's interest perked up at the sound of a female heroine story. "Tell us from the beginning, like how did they meet?"

Again, Eunhae went into spasms of laughter. "No, not like dat." She said waving the hand without the knife as if to erase Maddie's last words.

"Doje dayj…" Eunhae began. Maddie looked at me for help.

"Those days?" I interpreted.

"People know each oder apter dey marry."

"But what brought them together?" Maddie asked.

"Snakes."

"Snakes? Or snacks?" I volunteered since many of my ESL students had problems distinguishing those two words.

Eunhae responded by zigzagging one curved hand in a slithering fashion.

"When was this?" Maddie asked still trying to comprehend what snakes had to do with marriage.

Eunhae didn't answer right away as her brows furrowed as if calculating some impossible math problem. "I tink maybe nineteen twenty-pibe? My grandpader waj born in nineteen hundred one. I tink he waj twenty-pour or twenty-pibe when my grandpader got married."

"So 1925? Where?" persisted Maddie like a reporter.

"In de countryside near Pusan. Hij pader waj parmer."

"Farmer?" I asked. "That sounds so nice."

Eunhae squirmed a bit at my idealism of farm life and quickly added, "No, my grandpader didn't want to be parmer. He want to study. But hij pader waj so - ..." She paused and demonstrated the missing word by squeezing her index finger and thumb tightly.

"Oh-um-stingy?" I guessed while Maddie blurted out, "Tight wad?" almost at the same time.

Eunhae slapped her hands together and nodded. "Yes! He waj so stingy he won't pay for my grandpader to go to unibershity."

"What did your grandfather do?" asked Maddie.

"He sabed all hij money and went to unibershity in Japan."

"Wow, he went to another country?" Maddie was impressed.

"Well, doje dayj Japan took ober Korea and occupy por tirty-pibe yearj."

"What? I didn't know Japan did that," Maddie exclaimed. While most people try to hide their ignorance, Maddie almost flaunted it.

Eunhae smiled compassionately. "Itj okay. I study really hard for my citijenship test ten yearj ago. But my good priend who libed here all her lipe, she didn't know her own history. So how can I expect you to know my country'j history?"

"Okay, so how did your grandparents meet?" I intervened as I could see Maddie's mind was swimming and probably her thumbs were itching to do a search on all the countries Japan occupied during the first half of the twentieth century.

"One night, when my great-grandparentj were sleeping in deir little parm house, my grandpader had a dream. He waj tinking about hij oldest son studying in Japan."

Suddenly, Eunhae reached over and grabbed my arm and shook it.

"Ah!" I cried out, dropping my apple slice.

Eunhae's eyes twinkled and added, "It must have been like that when my great-grandpader woke up my great-grandmoder."

We listened intently, filtering out her strong accent. Through our imagination we were transported to rural village in Korean in 1925.

***

"Wife! I had a dream. Tell me what it means."

"Hmm? What is it now? What's the matter? I was in such a deep sleep…"

"In my dream, I was walking home from the rice field like I do every day. But I was disoriented and haunted by an eerie silence. Then two white snakes appeared out of nowhere and started to follow me. I kept

walking, keeping an eye on them. They slithered right to left, right to left. Then one went to the west gate at the edge of town, straight to the herbalist's house – you know, the acupuncturist – what's his name?"

"You mean Mr. Lee?"

"Right, that guy. The one snake went right into the house and then the other climbed right up my leg and into my shirt – right HERE!" he said, thumping his chest.

"Did you say white snakes?"

"Yes, white."

"A white snake is a good omen. Two of them must be doubly good."

"So what does it mean?"

"It means you should go back to sleep," the wife stated decisively and rolled over. "Then in the morning you should go see the herb doctor just like in your dream."

"Why? What does it mean?"

"Well, before you fell asleep, you were worrying about our oldest son."

"Yeah, what was he thinking leaving a good life of farming to go study in Japan? He could make money right away! Instead, he saved all that money to spend it at a university!"

"Enough already! You keep saying the same things over and over. Don't you see he's different from you? Anyway, I think you're worried that he's not married yet. That's why you had that dream. So ask the herb doctor (yawn) if he has a daughter. I think he still has another daughter who's not married yet."

"But I thought she was old already."

"But our son is older and he's not getting any younger. Now let a body sleep!"

"But are you sure? We could hire a matchmaker."

"But you didn't want to pay a matchmaker. If you don't want the herbalist's daughter, you can sell your dream to Mr. Kim. He's always buying someone's dreams."

* * *

Suddenly, a phone rang and we were pulled out of time past.

"Oh, I porgot," Eunhae exclaimed startled. "Today ij Tuejday and my daughter callj me." She quickly answered her cordless phone. "Hi Jenna, I call you right back."

Maddie and I got up to leave our host. Eunhae started running from place to place in a whirlwind of activity then presented Maddie a plastic bag with a glass jar filled with reddish colored vegetables.

"Oh! Thank you so much," Maddie replied like a surprised prize recipient without an acceptance speech.

"Put in pridge apter pew dayj."

We waved our goodbyes and hurried out so that mother and daughter could have their weekly meeting.

"I can't believe they met because of a dream," Maddie said trying to process what she just heard.

"Why? You met Brian on the internet. Dream, internet, matchmaker...what's the difference?" I said insouciantly.

"What? We chose to meet each other. Besides, I didn't meet with him until *after* I found out we were actually in second grade together. He wasn't a total stranger."

She sounded rather defensive so I just dropped it.
It was the first time that I saw Maddie deep in thought.
She mindlessly placed the kimchi bag on the kitchen counter and quietly retreated to her room and closed the door.

When I went to bed that night, I thought I heard a small POOF sound in the kitchen.

3 Birthday Soup

"Maddie! MADDIE!" I cried out more shrilly than I
intended. The pungent smell of kimchi bits that were
strewn all over the kitchen counter had entered my nostrils
and the garlic, onions and ginger began a war inside my
nose. I panicked.

Maddie shuffled out of her bedroom, still in her pajama
pants and t-shirt with her cellphone in one hand and
rubbing her eyes with the other.

"What's up?" she asked yawning. "Oh, what happened?
The kimchi...OMG...the kimchi exploded!" Her eyes
widened analyzing the aftermath. Then she laughed and

snapped a couple of shots of the disaster with her phone.

"That's well and good but you will clean it up, right?" I said firmly without seeing any humor in the situation.

"See, last night I got hungry and saw the kimchi here so I ate some, well, okay half the jar. And then the jar looked too big for what was left so I put it in one of your plastic container thingies that has that snap lock. I had to force it shut but it was the right size..."

"You put a fermenting thing into one of my plastic containers?" I said trying to suppress my irritation.

"Yeah but see?" Maddie said, "I remembered what you said and I washed Eunhae's jar and put a couple of chocolate mints inside so we can return it with something."

"Kimchi-flavored chocolate mints?" I looked at her incredulously.

"No worries. I'll clean it all up," Maddie assured as she picked up one of the kimchi pieces and ate it off the counter. "Ooooh! And know what? I got a new fan on my food blog!"

Maddie looked at her phone and made a few taps and held it up to my face.

"Such a delicious description, Global Girl!" I read straining to see the writing on the tiny screen. "Who said that?"

"That's what's cool. I don't know him. He read my latest entry about Eunhae's kimchi and almost immediately, that comment appeared!"

"How do you know that LoneStone is a guy?" I inquired.

"No girl would choose a name like that."

"Well, I don't know about that. But please, clean this up before I get home. I can't have breakfast here. I'll just grab a granola bar and go. I don't think I can stomach anything with that smell."

I grabbed my backpack, water bottle and car keys and in a spur of the moment decision, I picked up Eunhae's jar thinking I could delay coming home for just a bit longer. I left muttering to myself, "what a great way to start a birthday."

Three hours later, around noon, just as I had planned at the start of this unsettling day, I stopped by at Eunhae's to return her jar. She came to the door quicker than I expected.

"Itj your birtday! I must make you birtday soup!"

"But how did you...?"

"Maddie came this morning and she tell me about de kimchi." She covered her mouth with her hand and stifled a laugh. "So sorry. Sorry. She not know to not put too much kimchi in container when still permenting. She sayj itj your birtday."

I then recalled muttering to myself about the birthday when I left. I realized that Ms. Chatterbox also has radar hearing.

Eunhae grabbed my arm and pulled me inside her house. I intended to stop by a few minutes to drop off the jar which contained the kimchi-infused chocolate mints. I

didn't want another gastronomic adv[...]
that I was. All I wanted was a brief d[...]
heading home. I felt I needed a nap
where half the students were cough[...]
my tiny neighbor's physical streng[...]
of persuasion.

"Tanks por bring back my jar," she said as her voice [...]
behind her into her bright, warm kitchen which smelled of
peppers, roasted sesame seeds and fresh fruit. I was about
to correct her English but decided it would be
unsuccessful.

"On birtdayj, we habe to habe sheaweed soup."

"Seaweed? Why?" I wondered if she sensed a certain
pleading in my voice.

"Sheaweed ij srippery and remindj ob being born. So about
time to gibe birt, pregnant women habe dis soup so baby
coming out smoodly and eajy like dis srippery sheaweed.
Plus, new moderj eat dis soup becauje it so nutritious. It
haj -how you say- ayohdeen?"

"Iodine?"

"Yes, dat one," she confirmed pointing at my lips as if she
could read the word on them. Then she reached into her
cupboard and pulled out a long plastic sleeve filled with a
dark, blackish, dried vegetation that looked like the dried
remains of a forgotten bouquet. My head guessed dried
seaweed. My nose confirmed the smell of the sea as she
poured hot water over the vegetable which she had broken
into pieces. The water transformed the dried mass into
broad leaves that looked like they were coming alive and
swimming.

We go por walk," instructed Eunhae.

...d nothing as I knew that this part of the soup making ...rocess was not in my control either. So we took a leisurely stroll around the neighborhood block as the autumn sun hid behind the clouds.

"Itj sad you know," Eunhae suddenly volunteered pensively. "Probably no one made sheaweed soup for my grandmoder when she had her pirst child."

"Why?"

"Becauje eberyone so disappoint."

"Because everyone was so disappointed?" I corrected subtly. "Why?"

"Becauje she had a gul. You know, eberyone wanted a boy and if de daughter-in-law had a gul, her moder-in-law waj angry. And ip she didn't scold daughter-in-law den she scold someone else like de maid."

"Whaaat?" I began to feel the hairs on my neck rise. Injustice does this but injustice against women, well...

"Sad, yah? Only sonj can get parentj' property, not daughterj. Daughterj had to libe wid deir in-lawj and become part of deir pamily. And to get dem married, you habe to gibe big gipt to in-lawj. So it was bad to habe daughterj."

"So that was your mom?"

"No that waj my mom'j older sister. My mom waj born in Nort Korea. Dat waj good, bery good por dem. Dey libed par away prom my grandpader'j parentj. No one got scold por my mom'j birth. Eben my grandpader helped aj midwipe."

"You mean midwife? What an interesting man!"

"Yes, he read many books and know lotj about many tings. We need such men to change peoplej' tinking. Need brabe women, too, like the daughterj of Sellobehase."

"Who?"

"You know in Bible, some women went to Mojes and said dat deir pader had no sonj but dey are hij daughterj so should get land, too. Dey want what God promised."

"Oh...Hmmm. Zelophehad? From the book of Numbers, right?" I inquired, mentally patting myself on the back for coming up with that obscure name.

"Maybe. I don't know how you call in English. But doje are good and strong women. They ask Mojes. Mojes ask God. God sayj, it ij good to gibe land to daughterj. That make good change por people."

"So if your aunt was born in South Korea and your mother was born in North Korea, what year did they move? Did people move freely back and forth then?"

"Dat's right, Risa. In doje dayj, dere waj only one Korea but it waj taken ober by Japan prom 1910 to 1945."

"So when did your grandfather move from his hometown to the north and where?"

"Dis waj in 1931 becauje my moder waj born in 1932 in Pyongyang."

"Oh. I remember reading about that year. In 1931, the Japanese invaded Manchuria. Some historians say this is when World War II really started."

Eunhae blinked a few times trying to digest what I said. I realized then that life lived in a time period doesn't guarantee knowledge about the world events happening outside of one's own small sphere of existence.

We arrived back at her home and then a tornado of activity commenced. I watched in awe from a safe distance. She slammed a few cloves of garlic down with her palm and pounded them with the side of a knife. The poor things had no choice but to give up their tight fitting papery skins which were quickly removed. Then the garlic cloves were swiftly chopped into an indistinguishable pulp. Meanwhile, a molasses-colored oil was heated in a large pot.

"What kind of oil is that?"

"Sesame oil. You cannot cook Korean pood widout sesame oil," she said authoritatively.

The garlic bits in the warming sesame oil filled the entire kitchen with a sweet, roasted aroma. Unlike some garlic smells which sometimes resembles burning rubber, this was really a warm, sweet and delicious smell.

Eunhae then poured some ready-made beef broth into the pot and brought it to a full bubbling boil. Meanwhile, she was back at the sink washing the seaweed which had now grown to ten times its dried size. It seemed to move like a live octopus. But with a few snips of a kitchen scissors, the multi-limbed vegetable was tamed, then thoroughly washed and gently added to the soup. She then added a can of something I did recognize, my favorite brand of chopped clams. When all was brought to a regular boil, she pronounced it done as she added a touch of soy sauce for extra flavor.

We sat across the table from each other, each with our own steaming bowl of soup with rice added. The bowls were accompanied by multiple little dishes full of kimchi and pickled this and pickled that. And she gave a blessing on the food which I didn't quite hear because I was adding my own prayer, "Lord, kill anything that's not supposed to be alive."

At her gesturing, I cautiously brought up a spoonful to my lips and tasted a delightful, comforting mouthful of broth with clams and a smooth slippery bit of sea vegetable. The smaller bits of seaweed were more like egg noodles and the thicker more twiggy pieces were more like al dente fettuccine. Then I paused to remember and give thanks for birth and strong women who ask for all that God wants them to have.

4 Love Among Enemies

"Surprise! Happy Birthday to you! Happy Birthday to you..." sang Maddie as she approached me with a slice of dense chocolate cake with a generous coating of creamy-looking chocolate frosting.

"Maddie... oh, how sweet. You really shouldn't have...I... just came from Eunhae's and tried some seaweed soup. I'm really full," I tried my best to back out of eating more new foods. I had just stepped in the door when I got this surprise. I hated surprises.

"I researched the recipe and found a dairy-free, gluten-free recipe which is just chock full of chocolate and it's soooooo good. You gotta try it," Maddie insisted. I confirmed this statement by looking around and not finding the rest of the cake. But thankfully, except for the dishes in the sink, it looked clean. The last vestiges of the kimchi explosion was masked by a lavender candle burning on the counter.

"So for sure there's no milk in the cake?" I double-checked with her.

"Not a drop."

I took a small bite and it was like eating chocolate pudding with chunks of chocolate chips barely holding together. Oh well, it was chocolate and I gave in.

Then Maddie regaled me with her visit with Eunhae earlier. I ate slowly and listened. Maddie's third superpower just after eating and internet searching, was talking while hardly taking a breath. In the onslaught of words, it slipped my mind completely to ask her if she knew anything about a beat up old red Honda Civic in front of the house earlier.

"I went to see Eunhae while you were out teaching today. I let her know what happened with the kimchi and she laughed. Then I told her that it made you mad..."

So I nibbled cautiously on the cake as I drifted into their prior meeting as I listened to Maddie's detailed retelling.

***

"Eunhae, I think Lisa is a bit prejudiced against Korean foods."

"Maddie, eberyone has some - how you say - puhrejudis?"

"But it's not like racial prejudice, right?"

"Rashism is bad. But you know most people judge oder people becauje of how dey look or deir social class or what religion dey beliebe. People identipy in groups. One group do something bad to anoder group. So dat group hates de oder group."

Eunhae suddenly realized the conversation was longer than one should have in a doorway and pulled Maddie in.

"I make snack por you!"

Eunhae looked like a television chef with ingredients all available at her fingertips. She pulled out some roasted sheets of seaweed and placed it on a plate. Her computerized rice cooker sat like a guard on the counter, perpetually ready with cooked rice set on "warm." She spread some rice on part of the seaweed sheet and added a long slice of kimchi on top. Then she rolled the whole thing like a jelly roll. Next the roll was sliced into perfect little rounds which she placed on a plate before Maddie.

"Ooh, thanks! It's like kimchi maki sushi."

"Well, in Korean, we call dis kimbap. 'Kim' por sheaweed and baaap por rice," Eunhae explained making the second pronunciation extra-long for Maddie to hear it right.

"So Koreans and Japanese are like the same people, right? So why do some Koreans get offended if I mistake them for a Japanese person?" Maddie inquired starting to devour the kimbap. Suddenly, she started to fan her mouth. At this motion, Eunhae quickly got her glass of water to put out the fire in her mouth.

Eunhae looked deeply and seriously at Maddie after she had recovered from the heat.

"Maddie, what ip some people come and kill your pamily, and tell you dat you are inperior person, make you speak deir language only and porce you to bow down to deir gods. How you tink, Maddie, ip dat happen to you, would you lobe doje people?" Eunhae cocked her head to one shoulder and peered at Maddie like a bird and waited for her reply.

"Um. I guess it would be really hard to love people who did that," reluctantly confessed Maddie. "But the Japanese people are really cool. They have wonderful art and literature and samurai movies and fabulous food so you can't hate all those people!" she added passionately.

"Dats good point, Maddie. My moder agree wid you. She went to school during time Japan take ober all Korea. She already could read and write in Korean but when she start school, it waj all in Japaneje."

"So can she speak Japanese fluently?"

"Yes, and she learned so much about Japan and deir culture. And she really lobed her teachers. All of dem were Japaneje."

"So the Japanese teachers really liked your mom even though they were like enemies because of politics, right?"

"Yes. Dey gabe good gradej but could not gibe her pirst prije."

"Why? If they thought she was the best student, she should get first prize."

"Yes. But dey taught Japaneje people are better than all oder people especially Koreanj. So dey alwayj gibe pirst prije to Japaneje student. My moder alwayj got second prije."

"Really and yet your mom still likes Japanese people? You think it's because she learned to appreciate their culture?"

"Yes, my mom can aboid buying Japaneje carj and products but she alwayj had good Japaneje priendj who lobed her, too."

"How about your grandparents? What did they think about the Japanese after they took over Korea?"

"My grandpader was ten when Japan occupy Korea. He went to unibershity in Tokyo when he waj maybe 19 and worked hard to pay por college. He deliber newspaper. At dat time, in 1923, waj a terrible eartquake. Apter eartquake, lots pirej all ober Tokyo."

"Huh? What's 'pirej?'"

"You know de ting dat burn."

"Oh, fires! Got it."

"When bad tingj happen people blame someone. So Japaneje said Koreanj caujed pirej. So dey killed around 6,000 Koreanj libing in Tokyo at dat time."

"What?! 6,000 people!!" Maddie's eyes bulged.

Eunhae calmly nodded. "When deje people came to kill my grandpader, hij boss stopped dem and protected him becauje he really knew my grandpader. So you see, eben when groups ob people hate each oder, dere can be lobe between indibidual personj."

Maddie nodded a few times then perked up. "But what about your grandmother? Did she have that good experience with any Japanese person?"

"No. To her dey are really bad. Becauje she neber got to know any personally. Por her, she most hated dat dey porced people to bow to deir Shinto shrine. Dey also put deir godj in church."

"So were there a lot of Christian churches in Korea then?"

"Yes! In 1907, dere waj big rebibal in Pyongyang and so many people became Christian. When my grandparentj libed dere, Pyongyang had many Christian churchej. De one my grandmoder went to had pamous pastor named Ju Ki-Chul. Japaneje tortured and killed him becauje he don't deny Christ. Hij wipe waj my grandmoder'j good priend but she died of breast cancer. Apter dat, my grandmoder no longer want to libe in Pyongyang."

"So is that when they left North Korea? Was that before or after World War II?"

"Apter. Let me tink. Aj soon aj Japan surrender and second world war ended…" Eunhae tapped her right forefinger on her chin and seemed to do some mental calculation.

It only took that brief silence for Maddie to rapidly search the internet on her phone.

"What the … I can't believe this!" Maddie cried and showed her phone screen to Eunhae. "It says here that just *two days* after the Hiroshima bombing, the Soviet Union declared war on Japan and invaded Manchuria."

"Really? So past? I know dat Sobiet Union inbaded Manchuria and came to Korea. It happened so bery past so US had to quickly set de 38th parallel to dibide Korea into Nort and Sout or else Sobiet Russia would take all Korea."

"Wow! What a change from one government to another. What did that mean for your grandparents?"

"Pirst dere waj a bery short celebration becauje it pelt like dey are pinally pree! But de sobiet communists took ober school where my grandpader waj principal. He don't agree wid dem so he had no job. Two yearj apter dey pinally decide to leabe."

"Such a change from one terrible oppressive government to another. Still, I'm impressed that your mom has such a high opinion of Japanese after all that," mused Maddie.

"Dis kind of ting ij not new. Hate between two groups of people happened long bepore dere waj any such ting as 'country.' We read in Bible about Naaman. Syria and Ijrael were enemiej. But Naaman waj great Syrian general and he beliebed in God ob Ijrael apter meeting wid Elisha. And in Jesus time, Romanj and Jewj hated each oder but some Jewish people lobed a Roman centurion and asked Jesus to help him. So eben among enemiej, indibidual people can lobe each oder."

***

Maddie grew silent as if reflecting on their conversation again but when our eyes met, she asked in alarm, "What's wrong, Lisa? You look kinda green…"

"Perhaps it's something I ate," I managed to say as I felt a battle starting in my stomach and hurried to the bathroom. Miss Talkative followed.

"Um, Maddie, I'd really like to be alone in the bathroom." I pushed her gently out the door. But she continued talking through the door.

"But why do you always blame food?"

"Because all my life I struggled with stomach issues. I couldn't leave the house without anti-diarrhea medicine. My mom said I had a nervous stomach. The doctors at least found out I have lactose-intolerance. There really wasn't any milk in the cake, right?"

"No! I used butter in the frosting but no milk."

"Maddie, where does butter come from?"

"Uh---ooops."

I heard her head thunk against the bathroom door a couple of times.

5 Bone Broth Soup

I don't remember much after I stumbled out of the bathroom and Maddie helped me into bed. The next day or two passed by in a blur. I think I slept through most of it except for the times Maddie woke me up to see if I was still breathing. Poor gal probably thought she killed me. I didn't get to explain that I probably got some virus at work. Most of the students in my class were coughing and sneezing. It wasn't until a few days later that I got the full story about how Eunhae's help was enlisted in finding a cure.

***

Maddie went over to Eunhae's house and rapped urgently on the door.

"Maddie, what's matter?" Eunhae asked looking alarmed when she opened the door to see Maddie's desperate face.

"Eunhae, what do you need to eat if you haven't eaten for a couple of days? You know, something that can help regain your strength?"

"Well in de last yearj ob my grandpader's lipe, my grandmoder made bone brot."

"What's that?"

"Well, you boil some cow bonej."

"Cow bones? What part of the cow?"

"Well cow peet ij best."

"What? Peet? Oh, cow...feet? Where do I buy that?"

"You can buy tail bonej ip you cannot buy peet."

"Okay, I think I saw something called ox tails at the market. Then you boil them ...?"

"Yes, Boil for porty-eight hourj..."

"WHAT? She's sick now. I don't have forty-eight hours."

"Just one minute. Let me tink.... I remember I have some seollantang in the preejer."

"You have some already made in the freezer?"

"Yes. I can warm it up and gibe you some, ok?"

"Oh, that would help so much. Thank you, Eunhae!"

Maddie rushed in without an invitation. "Anything I can do to help?"

Eunhae was quite surprised at how at home Maddie was after just a couple of visits. But she welcomed the opportunity to exercise hospitality and set the electric kettle to boil for tea.

"Maddie, I want to ask you. Dere waj a red car in pront of your house dis morning. Did you ..."

"Red car? What kind of red car? Did it have a gray patch on one side?" Maddie looked startled.

Eunhae observed the sudden change in Maddie's tone of voice, "I only saw prom my house. I don't see gray patch."

"No way...." Maddie said as her eyes grew distant.

Eunhae quickly directed her into the kitchen to bring her back to reality.

"I'll rook por the bone brot and any oder soup to uje," Eunhae said rummaging through her fridge. "Oh, here ij presh green onionj. Can you pleaje wash and chop?"

"Okay!" Maddie said with enthusiasm finally able to do something tangible toward helping Lisa.

Eunhae took out two big plastic containers from the freezer. She put them to defrost in the microwave. Then transferred the mostly thawed broth into two pots on the stove to simmer.

"How did you make the broth?"

"Just boil por looong time. Need higher boil not just

simmer or it doej not turn white like dis. Dis white color come prom bone, calshium. It really help ip someone haj no appetite."

"But how can you cook something that takes so long when you want to eat now?"

Eunhae laughed and playfully hit Maddie on the shoulder.

"No microwabe in my grandmoder's dayj. She tink ebery day what to cook tomorrow, maybe what to prepare next week or next mont. She had big pamily. She had to go to outdoor market and argue wit seller how much to pay. Ebery seller knowj her. By time she was ninety, no one argue wid her. Whateber she want to pay, dey gibe her dat price."

"That's funny. Bet she got better deals than any coupon clipper! But today who has that kind of time?"

"Itj not just time, Maddie. Itj lobe. When dere ij cabbage in de market, she tinks how much kimchi to make por whole pamily all winter. Ip someone ij sick, she haj to make some kind ob soup. She alwayj planj tinking how to peed whole pamily. Planning, cooking pood ij her way of showing lobe."

"How big was the family?"

"By de time dey get ready to leabe Nort Korea, dere were six children and she waj pregnant."

"What? How could they even think of escaping with so many children?"

"My moder and her broder lept pirst wid church priend. Den my grandpader and grandmoder hire boatman to moobe big tings. Boatman say he not take grandmoder and she must go wid children alone."

"What? That's not right! Who would send a pregnant lady on a life-threatening journey with four children? What was your grandfather thinking?"

"Yes. Dey bery scared. But dey habe pait."

"Faith?" Maddie wondered how much faith was needed to undertake such a harrowing journey with four children. "How old were the children?" she asked.

"De oldest waj 18 but she had tube-ku-lo-sis - someting like dat."

"Tuberculosis? Oh no!"

"Den my second oldest uncle was ten and hij two younger sisterj were seben and pour."

"Did they walk all the way?"

"Oh, no. Dey took de train prom Pyongyang to Kumkyo."

"How far is that? From Pyongyang to Kum-what?" Maddie couldn't resist anymore and started tapping on her phone to find the North Korean cities.

Eunhae furrowed her brows and thought hard. "Mmm. Maybe 85 milej? You know, my grandmoder wrote Kumkyo in her diary but I tink she meanj Kumchon."

The bone broth bubbled in the background while Maddie followed Eunhae's story of her grandmother's impossible journey and lost herself in the story.

***

It rained all night and the crowd of travel-weary, rain-soaked passengers were emptied onto the platform to be subjected to inspection. It took hours. Each person had with them what was dearest. Everyone knew the others were trying to escape.

"We will summon you one by one for the inquisition!" blared a loudspeaker at five in the morning.

The inquisitor was an average sized, clean-shaven man in a heavily starched uniform. He glowered with menacing eyes at the small woman. Perhaps he was once a street vendor or an unsuccessful opera singer because the first thing he did was to shout projecting his voice to the other end of the station.

"You are trying to run away to the south aren't you?"

"Yes, we are," she answered immediately.

At first, he was taken aback by her forthrightness, but recovered quickly and sneered. "You were going to Seoul because your husband was settled down in Seoul already and sent for you, isn't that right?"

"That's not so. I have to go because I was originally from the south and our parents and children are there. Please let us return home." If he had listened carefully, he would have recognized her strong southern accent and would have known that it was the truth. But he continued shouting and using abusive language. Furthermore, his co-workers also joined in yelling and belittling the middle-aged mother.

Something started welling up inside the well-

mannered lady. Perhaps it was brewing during the long night waiting in the rain, soaked to the bone, worrying about her children's health. She looked at these Korean communists more loyal to "mother Russia" than to their own people having been brainwashed by the Soviets.

"Leave your North Korean citizen's ID now and get back to Pyongyang!!" several officials yelled in chorus.

She threw her ID at them and shrieked with a cracking voice, "I don't need this. We have no place in Pyongyang to get back to! We have to go even if we die trying!"

"I don't care if you die!" the first inspector spewed out hatefully.

"Give us back our handbags!" she demanded.

"Your stuff now belongs to the state governed by the people!" the investigator growled baring his teeth like an attacking bear.

"Don't bother us anymore!" she motioned for the children to get moving.

The family, overcome with fatigue, checked in at a nearby inn and ate some soup and rested. That evening, the inn's owner approached them.

"Ma'am, do you have ID?" he asked in a polite business manner.

She remembered she threw it at the inquisitor early that day and nervously replied, "No."

"I'm very sorry but you have to leave."

"What? Why?" she searched his eyes for compassion. "Please let us stay at least until morning since it is difficult to look for a room in a strange town in the night with four children."

"No, I'm so very sorry but if I house any person who does not have an ID I will be fined and my business will be suspended. Tonight an inspector is coming. I'm really very sorry." He apologized once again but he seemed quite determined about his refusal.

Numb with disbelief, Eunhae's grandmother herded her children out into the street where they huddled together. To make matters worse the rain would not stop. Her oldest child began to sob softly at the utter helplessness of the situation.

Ambling aimlessly the weary mother quoted a familiar verse, "Foxes have holes and birds of the air have nests. But the Son of Man has nowhere to lay his head."

A young man, who was wiping a car, watched them carefully. No one considered how odd or futile it was for someone to be wiping a car in the rain. He stopped and approached the family.

"Ma'am, where are you going?" he asked.

"We are going south." she answered without passing the information through a security filter.

The stranger's voice was gentle and his eyes were kind.

"Sir, would you help us find a place to stay?"

"Why didn't you check in a motel?" the stranger inquired.

"I don't have an ID," she confessed not giving the details of how she lost it.

The young gentleman seemed to be thinking about something and left.

"Oh, Lord, please provide us a place and protect us," she prayed.

A little while later, she heard the innkeeper calling from around the building in a pleasant tone, "Ma'am, please come back."

Suppressing suspicions, she hurried the children back to the inn. The young man, who was wiping the car outside, was sitting on the porch of the inn.

"Ma'am, do you really have to go south?" he asked scanning her face for sincerity.

"Yes, I have to. Our parents and two other children are there," she said only repeating what she said early that day to the inquisitor.

He sighed. "There are some people who need to go but many others are going without reasons." He wrote a note on a piece of paper and instructed the innkeeper to send someone to the station and get a voucher to allow the family to remain at the inn. A person at the inn did so and brought a certificate along with the confiscated baggage.

"Oh, Lord God," Eunhae's grandmother prayed silently. "You are indeed so gracious! Thank You that You never abandon us or forsake us!"

The mysterious young man left quietly before Eunhae's grandmother could thank him.

"It is a very good thing they sent that investigator tonight. That young man is a branch chief of the investigating office," informed the innkeeper.

"Do you know this man personally?" she asked.

"Yes. He's the son of a church elder."

6 Rice Cake Soup

"Oh my! Maddie, you did good job chopping green onionj!"

Maddie beamed but wasn't really sure if Eunhae was just being polite upon examining the schnitzel fritz she created out of the long stems. It was then she noticed that Eunhae was working over two pots on the stove.

"While you chopped dat, I put some projen rice cake into halp ob brot to make soup por us."

"What are those white oval things? Frozen rice cakes?

How did you make them?"

"No, I no make it. Take too long. You make rice and mash and make long, skinny rolls and cut diagonal like dis so it becomej obal-shape. We eat dis kind ob soup on runal new year."

"What? What is runal?" asked Maddie as this time she couldn't guess Eunhae's word alteration.

Eunhae stopped and thought a bit and knocked on the side of her head. "Sorry my pronunshiation is bery bad. In Korean, dere'j just one letter for 'r' and 'l.' 'R' sounds are at the beginning and 'l' sound at the end so I conpuse a lot. Por ejample, I tell my priend to cook pish just little bit but I said to 'seal pish on each side' and she say to me, 'what you mean, Eunhae? Why seal?' Den I say, no, I mean 'searrr.'"

"Oh, so if you said 'runal' you really mean 'lunar.' Ah. Got it. But sometimes you say 'l' words just fine like when you said 'little' and 'love,' I understand it just fine.'

"Yes. Doje wordj I practice lots cauje my daughter corrects me. She say, 'Mom, don't say 'rub' itj 'loVe! I tink I say right but when I talk somehow my brain change de way my mout say it."

Eunhae smiled and looked appreciatively at Maddie. "Maddie, I'm so happy my accent not boder you. You alwayj show interest in my wordj. Tank you."

This last comment warmed Maddie more than any good soup could do.

Eunhae placed two steaming bowls on the table and set cucumber kimchi and cubes of radish kimchi in addition to the cabbage kimchi. Maddie was delighted. She took her first spoonful and tasted the thick, milky-looking broth. It was delicately sweet as if all the bone mineral goodness got fully dissolved into it. The rice cake was soft and chewy and tasted just like rice but a bit sweeter. Eating this soup with all the spicy kimchi proved to be a perfect match.

"So tell me what happened next? How did your grandmother take four children across the border?"

"Doje dayj border waj not guarded so much like today becauje Nort Korea waj not established until 1948. Sobiet Union came to Nort Korea aj soon aj Japan lept. Dey set up temporary gobernment. Prom 1945 to 1948, around 800,000 people escaped to Sout Korea where de US helped to establish pree gobernment elected by de people. So at dat time, guidej made lotta money helping people escape prom Nort Korea."

"So your grandmother had to hire somebody to help her? How did she know who to trust?"

"You are so right, Maddie. How could she know who to trust?"

Maddie slowly enjoyed her soup and listened intently. This time she could hear Eunhae's grandmother's own voice.

***

While staying at the inn, we could overhear disturbing conversations.

"Did you hear about those wealthy people who tried to escape to the south?" one lady asked another.

"Yes, those horrid communists robbed them of all their lands and houses. They didn't even have enough money left to stay in a place like this."

"That's why they drowned while crossing the rough water!"

"Are you sure? Did they find the bodies?"

"Yes. Quite sure. They found nine bodies."

Three rainy days stretched into one endless period of gray. HuiJeong was coughing more, and constantly looking southward, as if her gazing could somehow expedite our journey. Every few hours, she would ask me, "Do you think Father made it safely south yet?" I had no answer for my beautiful firstborn, my daughter who was so terribly ill.

The river remained a formidable barrier in our journey. What was usually a nameless stream during the dry season, swelled above its banks due to the endless rains.

I needed someone to guide us and help carry the youngest. The chaos of war and the upheaval of governments gave birth to new entrepreneurs who helped numerous northern Koreans escape to the south. Some were honest hardworking people. But some stole people's money and goods and even murdered those who hired them. Still others were spies for the communist government taking the money and turning the people over to the police for even more money. How could I choose the right guide to help us?

Lord, only You know the hearts of men. You not only know us but You hold our past, present and future in Your Hands. Please grant me a good honest guide to help us get home to the south.

"Hey, ma'am, you're headed south aren't you?" whispered a woman who was watching me. She smiled at me reassuringly. I nodded but didn't say anything.

"You will need a guide to help you. See that big guy over there? He's a good man and you can trust him," she confirmed with an emphatic nod.

Without other options, I took her advice. The man was tall and dark skinned with the build of someone who did heavy labor all his life. His face was riddled with pockmarks but his eyes were hidden by sunglasses so I could not get a good sense about his character.

"Are you a guide who can help us get south?" I asked.

"Yes," he confirmed confidently. "For the small sum of 3000 won, I'll take you and your children south."

He saw me hesitate and suddenly broke into a smile revealing some missing teeth. He removed his sunglasses. One eye was much larger than the other, giving him a comical expression as if he were winking.

Ah, but look at those ears! Those are nice big ears. That means he has a noble character. I never asked his name, so forever he became Mr. 3000 in our memories.

"Lady, I may not be much to look at but you can trust me."

"Agreed. 3000 won it is," I confirmed, relieved in having made this decision.

Around midnight we had a hearty meal, with lots of meat and rice. We would need strength and endurance for the journey ahead. We reached the stream at one in the morning. The sound of the rushing river reverberated like a stampede of wild beasts in the moonless night.

The guide went in first carrying my youngest daughter secured on his back. He held onto the hands of the next two older children so that they moved as one large creature in the blackness. He gave no indication of how the waters affected him but all the rest of us gasped a little on our first contact with the chill of the water.

In the dark, I could see the outline of the guide with the three children. The waters buoyed up the two children on either side when their feet could no longer touch the bottom. They looked like one large figure with wings walking ahead of us. Lord, You sent Your angel to guide us!

HuiJeong and I followed into the bone-chilling, black waters after him. I carried a bundle double-wrapped in large silk cloths. It contained all the money from the house sale. The river's cold fingers tried to pry off my shoes as I tried to steady myself on the slippery river rocks. Suddenly, the swift current grabbed my legs and pulled me down the racing river. Like an expert pickpocket, the river stole my bundle. I was

*briefly completely under water. HuiJeong heard me
gasp as I got my head above the surface. She turned
around and with superhuman effort and speed,
caught the bundle and me in one instant. She was
using strength I knew she really didn't have. She held
onto me in a life-and-death struggle with a hungry
river. In the end, the river had to settle for my shoes
instead of us.*

*The guide and my other children heard the
commotion we made. Mr. 3000 quickly placed the
younger children at the bank and came back for us.
His strong arms held us steady and helped us reach
the bank.*

*"Are you OK? Sorry I should have let you wait back
there and come back for you.*

*I'm very sorry," he apologized with sincere concern.
As I caught my breath, I remembered the verse from
Isaiah:*

> *"Fear not, for I have redeemed you; I have
> summoned you by name; you are mine. When
> you pass through the waters, I will be with you;
> and when you pass through the rivers, they will
> not sweep over you."*

*As we continued on land, my bare feet became
acquainted with each change in terrain. Ah – that
must be a pinecone, ow! a sharp rock!*

*"Ah-yah!" What was that? Something moved under
my foot!! Was it a snake?*

"What's wrong?" Mr. 3000 whispered loudly.

"I lost my shoes — in the river —- and now --I'm stepping on --all sorts of things -- on the ground."

"Oh, here, you can wear my slippers." He kindly took off his straw sandals. These were the type braided from the straw left from the rice harvest. I was used to wearing only the soft rubber Korean shoes. I tried to wear his large slippers but even after a few hundred yards, I felt a layer of skin being scraped away by the rough straw so I gave them back to him.

I focused my thoughts on the children to avoid thinking about my feet. On a normal day, there would have been complaints and multiple squabbles between the siblings. But in this moment of desperation, each child cooperated beyond what any parent could ask. Then I heard an exchange of hissed whispers. It was my oldest HuiJeong and my son, KapJung.

"No, you can't," she whispered almost scolding.

"Yes, I can. I'm ten years old, Big Sister. I can carry the backpack for you. You are too tired."

"You're ten years old so you can't carry it. It's too heavy for you."

"But I'm strong. I'm really strong. I helped Father carry the wood to build the house. You've been sick, Big Sister. Let me…"

"No. I said 'NO' and that's final," HuiJeong hissed.

HuiJeong turned behind checking to see if I were following. Even in the dark, I could see a brief flash of teeth in a broad smile. I could barely hold in my tears seeing the sacrifices of my children.

After four hours of walking, a ghostly gray dawn revealed the outline of sleeping cottages huddled together. It was a welcome sight. By noon, we arrived at a tavern and had lunch. Then while everyone was eating, I turned toward the charcoal fire and tried to dry the bundles of wet North Korean paper currency. I imagined every eye in the tavern was watching me. I was so glad to have Mr. 3000 there to watch over us.

"Hey, auntie, that's a lot of money there," a passerby observed. "You know, if you go south, your North Korean money isn't going to be worth anything. You should go exchange it. "

I thought about this unsolicited advice and it made sense. I stopped trying to dry the money and exchanged the wet northern bills for dry southern ones except for the 3,000 won to pay our guide.

We resumed our journey after a short rest. At a certain point, Mr. 3000, suddenly turned around and faced us with a very serious face.

"Hey, kids and you ladies," he whispered nodding toward HuiJeong and me. "You have to be real quiet like - like a mute choking on honey! Not one word, OK? This is the place they have the most guards. Hold your breath if you can!"

Despite our fatigue, we found new energy in the fear of being caught. Each step was restrained. Each breath was monitored. We walked silently, gingerly, as if we were trying to walk past a sleeping dragon.

This tense march continued for perhaps an hour but it seemed interminably long. Then we arrived in Noo-rook village -- to free land at last! We got a room in an inn and slept off our fatigued, sore muscles.

"Ma'am, now that we've arrived safely south, I need to go back," our guide informed me. "Could you please go with us to the next town?"

He didn't object. When we made it to Kaesong, I gave him the promised 3,000 won. I searched for something else to give him for the extra work he did, but he was gone. I didn't have a chance to really thank him for all his kindness. Thank you, God for the angels you charge to guard us.

We were admitted to the shelter for refugees in Kaesong. The Red Cross medics administered typhoid and cholera shots. I feared for my unborn child during the vaccination. Soon after, I was shaking with chills and an intense fever. I remember slipping in and out of consciousness.

***

"She was sick? Oh! I almost forgot! Lisa is sick and that's why I'm here!" Maddie blurted, pulling herself away from Eunhae's story.

"I not porget," Eunhae said, "I put a small container wid kimchi and a big container wid bone brot soup. Here I wrap it por you."

Eunhae stacked the two containers in the middle of a large, square scarf. Then she tied knots using the diagonal corners of the scarf, forming a handle out of the knots.

"Dis ij de way we used to carry tings in Korea. My grandmoder ujed scarp not bag por shopping."

"That's so cool!" Maddie marveled as she received the scarf now turned into a bag. "Thanks so much, Eunhae!"

"Bye, Maddie. Tell Risa, get well por me."

Maddie hurried home and was relieved to see that I was up, sitting at the table with a cup of tea.

"Lisa! You're up. Look what Eunhae made you. Bone broth soup!"

"Um, I'm not really into trying anything new yet."

Before I could say more, Maddie put a whitish-looking soup before me.

"Um, Maddie, no milk in this, right?"

"No, it's white because the calcium leached out of the bones being boiled for a couple of days. Try it! It's really good with some kimchi." She paused and quickly added, "But you can skip the kimchi for now."

I realized I wasn't going to get out of this so I tasted a spoonful. It tasted like absolutely nothing at all. But almost a hint of sweetness could be detected if nothing had a flavor. But it was comforting to have something warm on an empty stomach. And then I remembered my manners.

"Thank you, Maddie. I can't remember the last time anyone took care of me when I was sick." I meant it. Then added, "Maddie, did you see a red Honda Civic in front of the house?"

Maddie looked shocked. "Did it have a gray patch on the passenger door?"

"Yes... I think it did..."

7   Chicken Noodle Soup

"Unbelievable!" The word escaped my lips though I wasn't talking to anyone. I examined the plate which had an entire baked chicken wrapped in plastic wrap. I had it all planned out how I was going to have Eunhae over for dinner even though I had to work late that day. I had just one hour from returning home to getting dinner on the table. Then THIS happened.

The beautifully baked chicken looked as if it had been dunked into a tank full of piranhas. Then I noticed a small pink post-it note which said, "I'm sorry! Will buy you another chicken."

"How does anyone eat an entire chicken?" I muttered in exasperation. I put the carcass into my crockpot, added water, a clove of garlic, an entire onion quartered and set the crockpot on the highest setting and hoped for the best.

When I got home that evening, the house smelled of chicken soup. I was relieved that I would have at least something to serve. I started to boil water to cook some noodles while doing a 100 yard dash all over the house looking for things out of place. "Maddie's jacket, Maddie's sweater, Maddie's cooking magazines…" I named each and hurried to her closed door to throw them inside. What I didn't know was that Maddie was on the other side of the door just as I opened it so I ended up throwing all these things right at her.

"Lisa!" cried Maddie, skillfully catching most of her items.

"What are you doing?" She then tossed the whole armload of things on to her bed.

"Maddie! I thought you were out. Anyway, I'm hurrying to get ready for dinner with Eunhae. Didn't you say you were going out tonight?" It was the first time I saw her in a skirt and her face all made up.

"I canceled last minute. I wasn't really sure…Say, can I join you?"

"Sure. And you can cook some egg noodles to add to the chicken soup that I wasn't planning to make." I raised my eyebrows and gave her knowing look, hoping she got the hint.

Maddie paused and then grabbed her head with both hands, roughing up her long, auburn hair. "Oh! Soorry! It's just I was so stressed and I didn't know what to do."

"About what?" I asked, becoming little concerned. I started to automatically fold some of the clothes that were scattered here and there and made neat little piles.

"Remember the red Honda? That's Brian's car. He's been trying to see me but he didn't have the guts to come to the door. You know, he's the one who's been commenting on my blog -- the LoneStone guy. He wanted to meet tonight. But I was kinda getting used to being on my own. I was thinking, it could be okay to start fresh y'know. And now, he wants to talk and try to work things out."

"So you don't want to even give him a chance? You must have liked something about him to marry him in the first place." I put my nervous energy to making piles of books and magazines on the floor.

"What about you? You could have gotten married. Why didn't you? Yet you seem perfectly happy."

"But I'm not you. When all my friends talked about liking this guy or that one, I just couldn't relate. I never had that feeling. It may be odd but as St. Paul said, some people are born not inclined toward marriage. Well, not exactly in those words." I stopped tidying and looked into her eyes to see if she understood what I meant. She shifted her eyes away. That's when I saw the tear stains on her cheeks.

From the kitchen, the pot's mad, rolling boil got our attention. We both got busy to welcome Eunhae to our home and to thank her for all her kindness.

Eunhae arrived right on time bearing a fancy store-bought chocolate cake.

"Eunhae! You didn't need to bring anything. After all you did so much for us..."

"Oh, thank you for bringing dessert!" interrupted Maddie swooping in to relieve Eunhae of the cake. "And here on the table are your dishes and beautiful scarf," she added pointing to the Eunhae's things on loan like a docent in a museum.

"Hmmm! Smellj good," remarked Eunhae encouragingly looking at our meager fare of chicken noodle soup, last minute salad full of diced up pieces of whatever we could find in the fridge and slices of bread.

Eunhae tasted her first spoonful and pronounced it good.

"Mmm, not prom can. Real chicken soup!" Then she reached for the salt shaker and shook it vigorously into her bowl. That's when I realized I forgot to add seasoning.

"So Eunhae, Maddie told me the story of how your grandmother got safely to the South with four of her children. What happened next?" I asked to start some mealtime conversation.

"Wait a minute," interrupted Maddie. "Didn't you say your mother and her brother went first with a church friend? They were the second and third oldest children, right?"

"Yes!" Eunhae smiled. "You habe good memory, Maddie. Yes, my moder and her next oldest broder lept pirst."

"Did that go smoothly?" I felt like I might have missed some details in Maddie's retelling.

"Not quite," Eunhae explained. "Dey got caught and put in prijon. And deir priend, Mrs. Moon-Chan, she went to pind them. Dey asked de guard to permit dem to shee her and as soon as de guard turned away, dey ran aj past as dey could to de nearby restaurant. De tablej were only knee high as eberybody sat on de ploor. So my moder and uncle, dey hurried under de table and hid. De customerj all protected them and don't tell the guardj when dey came to look por dem."

"Oh my goodness! What a scare! Did your grandmother find out that they escaped okay?"

"Yes, dere waj no mail between de two countriej so people going back and port carried letterj by hand. My mom wrote a letter so my grandmoder knew she was sape."

"It must have been so good to be reunited," I observed.

"Yes, but it waj a big problem dat my grandpader did not come yet. They waited and waited. My grandmoder was so worried."

"How long did she wait?" Maddie asked.

Eunhae cocked her head to one side and thought about this, "maybe tree monts? Dey came sout in late spring so probably all summer she waited. She planted some beanj to try to keep actibe and worried all day ebery day. Pinally, she could not stand anymore and decided to go to Seoul to pind out ip somebody hear someting about grandpader."

"You mean she didn't live in Seoul?"

"No," Eunhae shook her head and added with a big smile, "my grandparents, deir hometown is really sout and in de countryside. Itj par prom Seoul closer to Pusan."

"Did she have someone in Seoul she could stay with?

"Yes, she had a good childhood priend who married a pamous pastor, Reberend In-Sun Jun. Hij church was Chang-dong Church, which during de occupation had a

Japaneje pastor. But when Japan lost war, dat pastor transpered church and all de properties to Pastor Jun."

"That's really interesting. I didn't think there were many Japanese Christians and you say there was a Japanese pastor in Korea?" I marveled.

"Yes. It made me tink, too. I wonder ip dat pastor waj more at home in Korea wit oder beliebers dan in Japan. What waj it like for Japaneje and Koreanj to worship togeder in doje dayj? I wonder like dat."

"That kind of thing is always something that warms my heart," I piped in. "I think even in the time of King David, some of his closest men were from enemy nations, men like Zelek the Ammonite and Uriah the Hittite, who joined Israel's army because they believed in God."

"But tell me more about Pastor Jun," Maddie interrupted to reel me back to the story from my digression into Old Testament history.

"Pastor Jun took ober de church and really helped many repugeej prom de nort. So my grandmoder stayed wid him and hij wipe while trying to pind out about my grandpader. She asked eberybody but nobody knew anyting. She eben wrote a letter and asked someone going back nort to deliber to grandpader ip he pindj him. Apter dat, she just could not go back to tell her children noting. She decided to go back to nort and look por him herself."

"But why?" I objected. "She had six children worrying about her plus she must have been really pregnant by then!"

"Wow," Maddie said dreamily. "She must have really loved him."

"No," Eunhae disagreed, doing her windshield wiper motion with her right hand. "I don't tink romantic lobe." She looked rather perplexed as if unable to describe what could have possibly motivated her grandmother to risk her life and making her children into orphans.

"What do you mean?" Maddie cried incredulously. "Of course she loved him. I mean, she had seven children…" I tried to kick Maddie under the table but only managed to graze her skirt. I raised my eyebrows cocked my head at her hoping she would stop.

"Itj more like dedication. Maybe shej tinking, how my children can libe widout pader? And she had bery hard time in her pader-in-lawj house widout her hujband."

"You mean her in-laws mistreated her?"

"Not quite like dat. My grandpader's moder died and hij pader was not tinking cleally. And grandpader'j sisters all had some problemj so dey depend on deir pader. Ip my grandpader ij dere, he can help and dey respect him. But dey don't respect my grandmoder. And all the children came prom nort so itj all a new place por dem and not comportable."

"But it's a safe place where she and her children are. How could she risk her life and her baby's life to go back?"

"Maybe eben impossible things can be possible. God probided. Sometimej when lipe getj hard, God gibej us just the right people at the right time."

Maddie and I listened and imagined what would it be like

to be worried sick, seven months pregnant and setting off on a dangerous journey.

8 Journey North

I call to You for You hold each new day.
Lord, protect my children and lead the way
Grant me strength and friends for the journey
Reunite our family, O Lord, I pray.

As I walked to the train station in the pre-dawn
bleakness, I recalled my last train trip to Seoul, two
weeks before. My second eldest daughter
accompanied me then. My heart ached because I had

burdened her with the responsibility of all her siblings. As the train left, she didn't let me out of her sight as if etching my face in the train's window frame into her memory. Would this be the last good-bye? She waved until the train's sharp turn abruptly disconnected our visual contact.

God, You know all things. You know where my husband is. I feel so strongly that I make this journey. Please keep him safe. I need to find him, Lord! Please go with me to find him. I have to face the dangers of the North again. My life is in Your Hands, God Almighty. Please direct my path and please protect my children and husband. I ask this in Jesus' name. Amen.

The gray horizon blushed pink when I reached the train station. The schedule showed the train to To-Sung was departing at 9:00. After a simple breakfast of rice and seaweed from a snack stand with some hot barley tea, I boarded the train to To-Sung. I leaned forward, my whole body tensed with impatience, as if to force the train to move faster. I had a mission to accomplish but the train chugged sluggishly until it finally stopped in To-Sung at 3:00 in the afternoon. This was the last and northernmost train station in South Korea.

There were about ten other people on the train, whispering to each other.

"Are you going north?"

"Yes, you, too?"

I followed the small crowd of strangers closely. One lady was looking at me knowingly. It was a look of empathy. Despite the cover of my loosely-fitting traditional Korean clothes, she could tell right away that I was pregnant. In that single instant as we passed that glance of mutual understanding, I felt the sisterhood of women. We knew each other's plight, from the moment of our parents' disappointment at our female gender to the ordeals of childbirth and childrearing. We shared it all in that one glance. She came alongside me and smiled.

"Are you far along?"

"Yes, about two more months to go."

"You're going to the North?"

"Yes, I have to find my husband."

"This is my second time returning back to the north. The first time I guided my son-in-law who's now working in Seoul. Then I took my daughter and her son down during the rainy season. Now I'm going back to bring down my son and his wife. I know the way pretty well."

I was amazed at this woman who didn't look much older than me. Her fair complexion was radiant like a full moon. Yes, she probably looked a lot younger than me in my condition of fatigue, worry and pregnancy. She was already a grandmother. I then remembered that I had my first child at the late age of 28 and now was expecting at 43. But this woman was telling me about how she was hiking back and forth to the north risking her life to help all her relatives. What amazing strength and courage!

"Aren't you afraid that they might catch you and imprison you? "

"No, I know that God is helping me. If you believe in Jesus, even an insignificant person like me can do all things because He gives me strength."

Hearing her say these things instantly cheered me up. Thank You Lord, for providing me with a Christian sister to accompany me.

Most of the other people were tradesmen who made a great profit by purchasing goods in the south and selling them in the north. There were so many things that one could not buy ever since the communists took over. We had dinner at a restaurant where the owner was well acquainted with these entrepreneurs.

I ordered some beef broth with soybean sprouts, rice and kimchi and drank several cups of roasted barley tea. My lady-traveling companion, Mrs. Song, had some spicy seasoned fish with her rice and kimchi. We ate leisurely waiting for the night to provide us cover. We noticed one of the travelers. He was obviously not like the black market businessmen. His shaven head, a typical student's crew cut, was all we could see.

"Young man, where are you from?" Mrs. Song whispered at the back of the young man. There was no response. He was either rudely ignoring her or didn't hear. She lightly tapped his shoulder. The young man leapt up from his seated position on the floor and turned around. The others, who noticed his acrobatic jump, laughed.

He was no more than 15 or 16 years old. His clear, fair complexion drew immediate attention to his large, dark eyes. His initial look of fear gave way to a blush of embarrassment and he bowed politely. Then he looked intently at Mrs. Song's lips and motioned for her to speak again. She repeated her question. He nodded and took out a small chalkboard and chalk from his pockets.

He wrote in a most exquisite handwriting, "Hwang-Hae Province."

Mrs. Song noticed that the young man didn't have much to eat so she insisted he sit at our table and offered some of her food. He gratefully accepted. But we soon discovered that our curiosity interrupted his eating. Each answer required putting down the spoon or chopsticks, to write on the chalkboard and then erase and write some more. We felt it was more important to feed him. I marveled at how well he communicated and wondered if he might be more pure because he always had to think carefully before he "spoke."

A single river served as the boundary line between the north and the south. We waited until 9:00 p.m. for low tide so we could cross more easily. At high tide, there were only two options – swim or drown.
It was another dark night, the last day of September by the lunar calendar. My heart started racing at the thought of the last cold, dark river crossing. My legs shook even before they felt the freezing water. But determination plunged me forward into the fearsome black waters, which quickly crept up to my waist. I hesitated but suddenly, I felt a hand slide into mine. It was my new friend, Mrs. Song. We crossed without any problem.

We maneuvered ourselves on the rocky, uneven ground, groping like blind men. Since we couldn't take the heavily guarded paved roads, we traipsed through the rice field ridges and furrows. Suddenly, there was a flash of light. A guard was walking by. We quickly crouched down in the wet rice field holding our breath until the light passed by.

The muddy earth was slick as grease, causing my Korean rubber shoes to slide unpredictably like a person just learning to skate. Shloosh! At times, I stretched out my arms just in case I fell. If I did, I wanted to avoid falling on my protruding front so that the baby would be safe.

At one time, we must have made too much noise as a flashlight approached, seeking us out, flooding patches of rice field with blinding light. The most experienced traveler in our group, our unofficial leader, directed us to a trench filled with water used for irrigation. We all lay down in that muddy water which was just beyond the reach of that menacing light for the longest minutes of the night.

We trudged about for what seemed like hours, meandering in a directionless manner. The deaf boy scampered to stay with the group because in the dark, he could not depend on his most useful sense.

Our leader stopped and turned around. This man had made numerous trips between the north and south so he was acquainted with all the most dangerous places.

"I saw a dead body here. See?" he whispered to us. "That place there you can see a spot in the ground.

Dead with a bullet through him. Probably got caught going south." He pointed at a spot in the road. We all gasped.

Water trickled down my wet clothes into my muddied shoes. With each step water and mud oozed up between my toes. The rubbing of wet feet in mud-filled rubber shoes emitted a rhythmic shyuk-shyuk sound, which I muted somewhat by leaning more on the toes. Yet this created a balance problem with my heavy belly.

But the greatest difficulty in walking was crossing through the thorny bushes and brambles of the steep mountain paths. Thorny brambles in the shroud of night were like hunched demons with long claws that slashed at my legs. Large rocks, like dead bodies, sprawled out on either side of the path. The energy born from fear, forced my legs forward desperately trying to keep up with the group. Blood dripped down from the wounds on my legs in warm, sticky streaks. I kept my face forward, focused on the leader, straining my ears to follow his steps. Somehow, we made it to the top of the mountain.

The leader stopped and said, "Now you are all on your own. This is as far as I'm going. Go in peace and may you reach your destinations." With that, he turned and left. We all sat down. One of the men pulled out a cigarette from his pants and attempted to light it with his shaking hands.

"Hey! Cut that out!" hissed another man. "Cigarettes can be detected from a distance! You want to get us all killed?" The anxious smoker tried to swing a fist at him but then threw his unlit cigarette on the ground.

Others murmured, "What are we going to do?"

"Do you think we should've trusted that guy? What if he's a spy and he's going to call the communist guards to get us?"

Tension and ill ease filled our hearts. So putting aside my own self-consciousness and fatigue, I said, "Let's pray." I didn't know who among us were believers other than Mrs. Song and myself but all bowed their heads.

"God, Who created Heaven and Earth. You are our Way and the Way-Maker. Please guide us safely to our destinations. Protect us and keep us safe during our journey. Give us strength and courage. In Jesus Name, Amen." A low chorus of 'amen' followed.

We trudged down a hill and were surprised to discover a railway. Climbing over the tracks, we stopped to check on our direction when we encountered our worst fear. Our eyes were staring right at the back of an armed Soviet guard with a lantern in his hand!

The frontmost person motioned all of us to go back. We held our breath as we backtracked as noiselessly as we could. This was only possible because the night air was filled with deafening cricket songs.

"Those Russian soldiers will shoot if anyone crosses the railroad at night!" one of our group members informed us when we reached a safe distance. Everyone became resigned to taking a more circuitous route.

Endless slopes of bean fields taxed my wobbly legs. Such an arduous uphill climb would have winded me even in my youth, but in pregnancy just breathing was labor. Finally, I couldn't force myself to go another step. The pine trees started spinning. Every joint and muscle cried out in pain. I collapsed under a pine tree.

"Please – you – go on – without me. I'll try to - catch up with you - in the morning." Of course, I knew I could never find the way myself but it was physically impossible to go on. They all silently looked at each other and then they too decided to wait there until morning.

Though I was exhausted, sleep eluded me on the hard, cold ground. Every little noise woke me. Leaves rustled. A pinecone fell. The baby squirmed and kicked in protest against the freezing ground when I rolled on my side.

Doubts crept into my mind. My only defense was to keep repeating the same prayers for protection, for healing, and that I could find my husband. God must have smiled at my most fervent prayers offered during the most difficult night of my life.

Dawn was heralded by a rooster in the distance. The morning light revealed that the hem of my skirt was all torn, fluttering like miniature flags. My legs were covered with deep cuts crusted with dried blood. I changed out of my bloody, muddy clothes behind the pine tree. But my rundown condition still betrayed the night's journey.

A new sense of urgency seized everyone else in our

motley group. They all sped away. But my legs would not obey me. So I fell far behind.

Passing a village, I saw a group of men sitting around a bonfire. They appeared to be some kind of self-appointed security team.

"Hey! Aren't you returning from the South?" they yelled in my direction. I kept silent, held up my head and continued walking, rather, waddling away, trying to preserve a sense of dignity.

I turned my attention to a man on an ox-cart.

"Please, sir, could you give me a ride?" He looked at me and a look of pity overcame his face.

"Where are you going?"

"I'm going to Kum-Kyo."

"I'm not going to Kum-Kyo but I can let you ride on the wagon for part of the way." He got off the wagon and helped me climb up the splintery, wooden cart.

The morning sun blanketed my cold body and the slow rhythmic steps of the oxen, rocked me to sleep. Images of my children and husband swept passed me. I saw HuiJeong in bed, lying wrapped up as if in a cocoon. Then she emerged slowly, the blankets became wings and she flew away like a butterfly. I tried to chase after her when I heard a man's voice talking to me.

"Auntie, you have to get off here. Auntie? If you're going to Kum-Kyo, you have to get off here."

"Oh…I'm sorry," I said. "Oh, thank you. Thank you so very much."

As I clambered down off the cart, I could just make out my train friend ahead of me. I forced each leg, leaden with fatigue, to move forward. With tremendous effort, I caught up with Mrs. Song. She stopped to wait for me when she heard me panting behind her.

"Come on, you can do it!" she urged me on. "Here, you should eat something.

You must be hungry after last night," she said as she offered me a rice ball. It looked good to me. But when she extended the round, white ball of sticky rice, the sharp smell of vinegar stung my nostrils. I shook my open palm in front of my face.

"In your condition, you need to eat to keep up your strength," she admonished as she finished the rice ball.

"I feel too sick. I don't dare," I replied. She offered her arm to lean against and we plodded together. As we began to move forward I saw a stream.

It was the very stream I first crossed with my children three months before with the very kind Mr. 3000! The raging waters of that frightening night could hardly be recognized in the bubbling water that only lapped my ankles.

You were a ferocious lion last time, now look at you; you're just a little kitten! What did you do with my shoes, you rascal?

The river was a babbling brook gurgling a happy water song. It was like an old friend. I stooped down carefully and took a drink from my cupped hands, trying to preserve whatever vestiges of ladylike behavior I had. The water was so fresh, cold and clean; it tasted sweet like the waters from the well of my childhood home.

The stream was a tributary to a river which flowed freely unaware that it now helped to divide a country. I took my time, because after the initial sting, the icy waters numbed the cuts and itchy mosquito bites and that was a welcome relief.

When we were still in the middle of the stream, a patrolman on the horseback called out to us, "Hey! You guys are returning early today!" He then instructed his patrol team member to investigate us. Just visiting the south was considered an act of treason.

They questioned Mrs. Song first. And she quickly replied, "I told you, I was just visiting relatives. Please let me go back home."

"Who knows what you've been up to down south!" the interrogator snarled.

"I've returned, haven't I? Please let me return to my house. What kind of activity do you think an old grandma like me could do?"

"Get over there and wait until we decide what to do with you and the entire group of you miscreants," he ordered.

"It's okay. God will help us get out of here," I reassured her, patting her arm, more to comfort myself than her. But as I said this, I began to feel a peace, thinking that perhaps God can even use this situation to get to Pyongyang sooner.

"What happened to the deaf boy?" she asked another of our companions.

"Oh, I saw him over there. He was writing on his chalkboard like crazy. Then they told him to go with somebody who was moving soybeans to the station." We all strained our necks to see if we could get one last glimpse of him.

"Hey, you ladies, want to come? We can escape out of here – there aren't that many guards. We don't have to go with them to the station," one of the tradesman whispered to us.

"You go ahead if you can make it safely," I said. "I still have to take a train to Pyongyang. I can't avoid them anyhow." So some members of our group were successful in escaping. The rest of us were taken on foot at a comfortable pace to the station.

We were packed into a small room like sardines. Fatigue weighed heavy on me as I hadn't eaten anything all day. The small throbbing that started when I first awoke felt like a hammer pounding nails into my head. Every movement of my head set off more painful throbbing in my head, eyes, and neck. There was not a single body part that wasn't complaining. We were pressed body to body against each other. It was all I could do to keep my empty stomach from reacting to the nauseating smell of sweat, bloody wounds and soured breath.

*"They lock up political offenders in that wall closet,"
someone from our group said. He pointed with his
head. I looked over as they dragged a man out and
shoved him into the wall closet, and fastened the
padlock.*

*A truckload of people was brought in. They were
probably escaping to the south. The guards
snickered, "One truck of wild boars delivered right on
time."*

*"We'll have some fun with those guys. Just lemme at
'em!" Those guards talked rudely acting like wild
animals, themselves.*

*My name was called around 7:00 p.m. My heart
started pounding, as I remembered the last
inquisition, when I was going south. Lord, please put
a guard over my mouth! I staggered on my sore,
unsteady legs over to the official's desk. I didn't even
bother trying to straighten my hair this time.*

*"What was your purpose of visiting the south?" the
examiner asked.*

*"I went to attend the funeral of my mother-in-law." I
replied. She passed away before I made it to the south
but it was a good response. No good Korean would
doubt that a dutiful child or even child-in-law would
risk life and limb to attend a funeral. It was
something you did no matter the cost.*

*He looked me over in my miserable condition and
suddenly had nothing more to ask. He even added,
"You have had a hard day." His eyes softened as he*

looked at me. He finished stamping some papers and he stood up and motioned for me to stand.

"You know, you look just like my mother," he continued casually as he walked with me to the accommodation camp. Oh dear, do I really look that old?!

They kept us for a week at an "accommodation camp" while they filed all the paperwork. They charged 600 won a week for paltry meals. For detainees who couldn't pay, the rice was rationed. At those outrageous prices, my lady companion and I shared our meals to save money. With my belly growing, my stomach had less room so an ear of corn was enough for my lunch.

Six days seemed like a lifetime. Throughout the nights we waited for the dawn. And with each dawn we waited for the night. At last, we were released from the camp. Since we didn't have IDs, the border officials gave each of a piece of paper that provided us access to all public transportation.

After arriving at the Pyongyang train station, my friend and I said our goodbyes.

"Take good care of yourself. I'll be praying that you will find your husband well and that you both get back safely to your children," she said as we hugged.

"Thank you. I'll pray for your safety too and your last trip down. Even if I don't see you again in this world, we'll meet again in Heaven."

I took the streetcar and looked at all the familiar sights that I thought I wouldn't see again.

Everything, from the church, the schools, and all the buildings looked run down and depressed. Finally, the streetcar entered the familiar streets of our old neighborhood. I pulled the chain to alert the driver.

I went to the house of Mr. Jin-Ku Kim at Nam-Moon (South Gate). If anyone would know where my husband was, he would. I opened the front door and as I entered I saw my husband sitting on a chair, looking thin and frazzled. My first reaction was relief and joy that he was alive!

"I have been looking out the window hoping that you would come," he said feebly when he saw me.

***

"WHAAAT?" Maddie suddenly jumped up from her seat. "How could he be there just waiting? What in the world?"

Eunhae and I looked at each other. I was also dumbfounded that Eunhae's grandfather was just sitting there waiting for his wife but I didn't feel as upset as Maddie. Before I could say anything, Maddie burst into tears, ran to her room, slamming her door shut.

I shrugged my shoulders and looked apologetically at Eunhae.

"I help you wid dishes," offered Eunhae.

"No need, Eunhae. I'll visit you later in the week after I find out what's wrong with Maddie."

9 Poor Man's Cake

"Maddie, are you okay?" I asked as I knocked on her door.

"I'm okay, Lisa. Come on in," a croaky, sniffly voice answered.

"What happened?"

"I just lost it when I heard that Eunhae's grandfather was just sitting there waiting after all that her grandmother went through to find him. I mean, Brian would never do something like that." She said looking at me as if for confirmation.

"Oh. I guess you would know. I don't know him."

"Yeah, I mean. I don't know how much her grandmother loved her husband but she was willing to risk her life. Don't you think he should have also? I'd probably never put myself in danger like that." Maddie seemed to get more and more animated so I looked around the room to see if there was any calming distractions.

"Yes, but you don't have kids," I said making neater piles of her books and magazines on the floor. "She did say it was for the kids. And you don't live in the middle of twentieth century Korea with all their customs and values. You are an independent woman and you don't think like she did."

"You're right. I chose to marry Brian," Maddie agreed as she started to hang up various clothing articles which served as additional bedding. "I knew he cared for me. But after a couple of years of living together and being used to each other, things got into a routine."

She paused for a bit, holding an empty hanger. "Then he buried himself in his work and I saw less and less of him. When we were at home together, he'd relax by playing computer games with his buddies online. We just started to grow distant..."

She turned around from the closet and looked to see if I understood. "I got the feeling that I was just one item on his life's checklist. Get a car. Check. Get a wife. Check. Get a promotion. Check," she said writing invisible checkmarks in the air.

"I'm not one to judge about marriage issues," I confessed. "But it seems you are wrestling with how you really feel about him now. Do you still have feelings for him?" I asked searching her eyes for the answer.

"That's just it," she said as she threw some of the clothes she just picked up back on to the bed. "My feelings go up and down from day to day. Eunhae didn't even know what feelings her grandmother had for her husband. She just had determination to keep her family together."

"And faith," I added.

"I guess," she said thoughtfully, petting one of her sweaters as if it were a cat. "I wonder if I should have done something more. We didn't face a calamity, war or adultery or anything earth shattering. We just lived bland, boring lives that weren't what we hoped for when we took our vows."

"Is it possible to re-discover what you hoped for?" I asked suddenly feeling like a marriage counselor.

"I'd have to swallow a lot of pride after all that was said and done that led to our separation…Taking back heated words and giving apologies are tough barriers to cross."

"Well, is it harder than walking back into a dangerous country seven months pregnant?"

Maddie laughed. It was such a relief to see her smile again.

"If you see Eunhae before I do, you have got to tell me

why her grandfather was just sitting there."

"I'm curious, too. But she'll want to know what happened to you. So what can I tell her?"

"You can...I guess, you tell her I'm considering getting back together with Brian. I'll call him tomorrow."

"OK. I promise I'll let you know what I find out. Goodnight."

As I closed the door, a sense of relief came over me and I planned my questions for my next meeting with Eunhae.

A few days later, I was knocking at Eunhae's door with some early daffodils that I picked from my garden.

"Oh, hi, Risa! So good to see you!" Eunhae exclaimed with her usual warmth.

"Here are a few daffodils."

"Dappodeelj?"

"Close enough."

"Tank you so much. I like dis pretty color. How ij Maddie? Did I say someting wrong?"

"No, she has been thinking hard about maybe getting back with her husband."

"Husband? I didn't know she waj married. She look so young. Wow. Datj good newj! I pray por dat."

At this point, she almost started a jig and clapped her hands. I had no idea this kind of news could have such an effect on someone.

Then I smelled something frying in the kitchen.

"Oh, I almost porgot. I'm cooking bin-dae-dduk. It meanj 'poor man's cake.' Last time Maddie waj here, she said you don't eat pork. This time I made begetarian style. I waj going to bring some to you but you came!"

"Oh, Eunhae, I didn't intend to stay for a meal…"

"Itj okay. It waj one of my grandmoder'j paborite recipej. She used to cook dis one but she had no stobe, just pire. Ober de pire, she put de cober ob a big iron kettle."

"Cover? What do you mean?"

"You know, how you say, rid?"

"Lid?"

"Yeah, dat one," she said pointing to my lips again as if she saw the correct word exiting. She doejn't habe pry pan like we do today."

I followed Eunhae into the kitchen where I noticed some aromatic pancake-like objects frying on the stove.

"What are they made of?" I asked, feeling my food anxiety rising.

"I soak mung beanjs widout skinj and blend togeder. Dat makej batter. Den I added garlic, green onionj, bean suproutj and some pernbrake."

"Some what?" I translated her "p" to an "f" and got "fernbrake" but still had no idea what she was talking about. So I quietly googled it on my phone while she was busy turning over the pancakes. My phone screen showed me a picture of ferns that I see all the time in a typical walk in the woods. People eat that? Even the deer don't eat those ferns! I didn't finish reading about the possible poisoning section of the article when Eunhae got my attention.

"We are ready to eat!" Eunhae motioned me to sit at the table as she brought a plate of the pancakes to me and showed me how it was eaten. She used chopsticks to break off a piece, dip it in a tiny bowl of soy sauce and ate it. I hesitated but as I had come to understand this was her language of love, I couldn't refuse. *Lord, help me digest whatever this is!*

The first bite started as with any fried thing, crunchy like well fried hash browns, then there was a pleasant flavor of sesame oil and garlic and the texture of cooked vegetables. Then suddenly, kapow! Something powerfully spicy and a little sour attacked my palette. I reached for the water glass to extinguish the fire.

"Oh, I porgot to say I added kimchi, too. Ij it too spicy por you?" Eunhae asked with some worry in her voice.

I blinked back the tears and nodded. I used my fork to skillfully dissect my pancake into the outer and the inner parts and continued to eat.

"What kind of man was your grandfather?" I asked hoping to divert attention from the mess I was making on my plate.

"Oh. He was bery smart. In pact, he came prom small parming billage but many of dem did not become parmerj but bery pamous people."

"I remember you said he went to a university in Tokyo and then became a principal instead of a farmer like his father. That's interesting."

"He lobed learning so many tings. Apter dey mobed to Pyongyang, dey didn't need a midwipe. He helped deliber hij own children. And he was always researching prom books." At this point, Eunhae became more animated and used her fingers to count her grandfather's numerous talents. "Dat time, dere's no Youtube or Google, he learned by himselp, how to cut hij children'j hair, how to make pants and shoej. He waj great at parming and carpentry, eben built a two-story house all by himselp..."

"He sounds so capable and smart. But how could he just be stuck in North Korea when his whole family was waiting for him in South Korea?"

"He probably had some problem. I tink itj called ...panic attack? Someting like dat."

"What was the cause of that panic?"

"Well, apter he paid the boatman who waj to take him and the big luggage sout, de boatman run away wit hij money. He waited and waited and cannot pind him. So he didn't know what to do. All de luggage waj like his lipe's sabingj and he could not just leabe eberyting."

"So he was stuck with all the stuff and couldn't go? But surely, after your grandmother arrived, they could take another boat and go. After all, stuff is just stuff. They were alive and needed to be there for their kids."

"True," Eunhae agreed. She closed her eyes as if trying to understand her grandfather's motives more. "You know, I tink he waj tinking all hij sabingj could help buy medicine for hij daughter. It wajn't just money. Por him, it waj hij children'j puture."

"I remember when you first came to the house, you told me that your grandfather was released from jail on some holiday. How did he end up in jail in the first place? I thought he was staying at his friend's house."

"Well, when he saw my grandmoder, someting happened inside. He suddenly pelt energy and direction and motibation. He mailed a large pootlocker ob heaby tingj to hij pormer student in Haeju and planned the journey sout."

"So dey got caught at the train station like when your grandmother was interrogated?"

"Yes," Eunhae nodded. "It waj a dipprent station. Dey waited apter de train stopped and went to the batroom to aboid getting caught. But my grandpader waj stopped."

As I listened to Eunhae's accounting of this part of the journey, I tried to imagine what was in the mind of her grandfather. I listened for his reasons as to why he did what he did and why he couldn't act when he should have. What was it like to be repeatedly forced into inactivity by fear?

10 Prison

"Taffy!" sang out the rice taffy man. The sound, like the song of the pied piper, drew children from all over the neighborhood. Each child happily exchanged a small coin for a delicious stick of sweet, chewy taffy. All except for one little boy, who salivated at the sight of the taffy, then refocused on his little coin and put it back in his pocket. He turned away from the taffy cart to the roar of laughter from the adults who were observing his odd behavior.

The sting of that embarrassment woke me. That memory, which had become legend in my family, came up in a dream once in a while. What does that say about me?

I was awake but my body wasn't. My body felt cast in concrete. No muscle obeyed me. I remembered that this strange thing would happen to me while studying in Tokyo. Certain that some unknown disease would kill me, I lost so much time to terror. But the herb doctor said some people experienced this paralysis before fully waking. Relax, just relax. Gradually, a wave of prickliness swept over each muscle. When mind and body awoke, I realized I was in a concrete cell. How did I get here?

Was it just the day before? We mailed my largest foot locker to my student's home in the port town of Haeju where we planned to escape to the South by boat. Without considering the consequences, I used my own name on the address. What was I thinking?

We left some of our possessions with our friends and planned on carrying some of our valuables by hand. But the problem was how to board a train since my wife had no ID. Her good friend, InSook Paek, visited just before we left. She learned of the predicament and immediately gave my wife her own ID.

"No! I can't take your ID," my wife protested. "You need this to live here."

"My citizenship is not of this world. You need this more than I do now." Her face glowed with peace and calm. "Don't worry. God will protect us." With that she placed the ID in my wife's hand closing her fingers over it. We feared she would join the many other Christian martyrs.

The next day, we boarded the southbound train to Ki-I-Po then exited through the bathroom to avoid the interrogation officials. We then boarded the train again to Haeju. All we needed to do was to pass the ticket gate without being stopped. She made it through. But as for me, my old enemy, Panic, assaulted me in full force. My heart raced and an invisible hand choked my throat as my body poured sweat.

"Now just answer the questions honestly and you can go wherever you want," the cunning official asked in a kind tone. "What is your destination? Are you headed South?"

"Yes," I answered shaking and wanting to believe him.

"You traitor!" The official took my ID and

confiscated all the money which had been exchanged to South Korean currency. He rummaged through my borrowed suitcase which to everyone's surprise had car motor parts.

"Oh-ho! You're a saboteur! What are these things? Were you trying to make a bomb?"

"No, that suitcase belongs to a friend... He's a car mechanic."

We were escorted to a detainment inn which was heavily guarded. In the morning, we were summoned and we could only watch helplessly as they tore into our luggage and the footlocker which was confiscated from the post office.

Then two of the officials forced me in a chair and repeatedly slapped and punched me. The sting of their violent hands was easier to ignore than the shrill shriek of my wife's voice.

"Stop it!" she cried out as she lunged toward the officials from the other side of the room. "What are you doing to him? How dare you treat him like that!"

My heart pounded and my entire body trembled when I heard one of them push her away. He sneered at her. "Your bookworm husband will stay in jail for three months and then he'll probably go to a labor camp for thirteen years. That's what happens to educated men who will not stay to build this new country!"

She was forced to return to the inn and I was locked in a cell. It just didn't seem right after all we've been through.

*Morning must have come, as I heard her voice again.
An involuntary smile lifted my cheeks. I imagined her
face, her perfectly oval, symmetrical face with eyes
like gently sloping hills. Her voice projected loud and
clear.*

"You let my husband out! He did nothing wrong!"

"No! Lady, you can't go there."

"Let me see my husband!"

"No, grandma, stay here. No visiting."

"Grandma?! Who are you calling grandma?"

"Ma'am, you really need to go."

*"He's freezing in there. Let me at least give him this
blanket."*

*I marvel at the lion's heart in this tiny woman.
Perhaps it's due to surviving a hard childhood. She
lost her mother during the birth of her younger
brother. Knocking on doors all over the
neighborhood, she begged nursing mothers to feed
the newborn. She had to drop out of school to help in
the home as her father squandered their wealth.*

*In the front office, a wooden desk screeched as it was
moved across the floor. Hurried feet scuffled.*

"Lady! You cannot go there!"

"You unhand me right now!"

Then the voice of one of the younger guards spoke in a lower voice to her. I strained to hear the conversation.

"Listen, lady, tomorrow is Chuseok."

"So? I don't worship my ancestors. I'm a Christian! Besides, my ancestral tombs are in the South."

"Shhhh!" then came some lower sounds I couldn't hear.

"Do you expect me to believe that?" my wife replied raising her voice.

"Trust me, please! Just go back to the inn and come back tomorrow."

"I WILL come back. And I'll keep coming back until you release my husband!"

The door closed. I reflected on how she could be so courageous. Perhaps it was her faith. It was that faith which ignited my faith in God. In our first years of marriage, I'd watch her reading her Bible, a gift from an American missionary lady. I read lots of ancient and modern literature but nothing struck me in the same way.

But belief just hovered in my mind. My heart craved "Someone" to thank when I observed the wonders of nature and the perfect way things worked together.

One day, she made a huge meal. My university days were full of meager meals of rice and maybe some eggs and sugar if I had it. But she was a gifted cook.

Ten different dishes graced our small, knee-high dining table. My eyes welled up at the beauteous array of three types of kimchi, tofu, spinach, sweet potato, fish, cuttlefish and rice. I had no choice but to bow my head in prayer to give thanks. I believed.

Years later, our home welcomed students who also enjoyed her cooking. These students, who were blessed by my teaching and her good food, stayed in touch long after their graduation. Even now, I dared to ask for their help in the time of my need.

But what about now? What do I believe now? Things were so good in the years before the communist takeover.

This farm boy became an honored school principal. Students adored me. Teachers respected me. Lord, help me to find my honor in serving You.

All my savings were gone. My father could not understand why I would pursue knowledge in books instead of investing labor in the fields for tangible rewards. But as a teacher and then a principal, I earned well and saved for our future. Help me, Lord, to find my security in You.

And all those books, those things I treasured so much were confiscated. Lord, help me to treasure Your Word above these.

Such were my intermittent prayers throughout the night in between moments of fear and worry. Lord, release me from the prison of my own fears.

The next day, the guards unlocked all the cells and I could hear them repeating to each prisoner, "It's

Chuseok so you can celebrate with your family. You are ordered to return by nine tomorrow morning."

11 Sprouts and Vegetables

"Oh, I porgot!" Eunhae suddenly exclaimed drawing me back from her engrossing story.

"What? What did you forget?"

"My beanj! Itj been already four hourj" she declared as she jumped from the table and hurried to the kitchen.

On the counter near the sink was a large black cloth covering something. She removed the black cloth to reveal an ordinary green plastic plant pot. Curious, I followed her to see what this could possibly be.

"What is that?"

"Soybean suproutj."

"Oh! You're growing soybean sprouts. I see mung bean sprouts in the produce section of the grocery store. But you grow your own. How nice!"

"Yes. Soybean taste dipprent prom mung bean. Soybeanj have nutty plabor."

"I didn't think bean sprouts had any flavor. But I'll take your word…"

"Look dere! Dey grow so past!"

"Is it hard to grow?"

"No, not hard but ebery tree or pour hourj need to gibe water like dis," she said as she let the water pour from the faucet through the planter pot. I could see a crowded bunch of yellow-headed sprouts standing at attention.

"Every three or four hours? People do need to work and sleep…"

"Yes, but itj best if you can do many timej. Like in lipe, just simply doing small tings regulaly can gibe good harbest. Like when two people lobe each oder, itj not de big tings like wedding, annibersariej dat make deir lobe grow. Just eberyday being dere, listening being paitpul, dat can help grow."

My mind wandered to Maddie and wondered if there was a parable here for her.

"Why do you cover it with that black cloth?"

"To keep the seeds tinking dey are underground and don't grow leabes."

I took the opportunity of the distraction as she placed the black cloth over the pot to ask what was plaguing me about her story.

"Eunhae, I have a hard time believing that the North Korean guards would just let their prisoners go because they wanted to go on a holiday."

"I know, Risa. But datj what my grandmoder said. Doje dayj, Nort Korea was still new and not organijed. Or maybe it waj just doje guardj in dat town only."

"But is Chuseok that important?"

"It waj really important to some people. People cleaned deir ancestor tombj and tings like dat. But I don't remember my grandmoder celebrating it. Today itj a really big holiday in Sout Korea. Eberybody goej to deir hometown and derej big trappic problem. But in Nort Korea, dey only start to celebrate Chuseok again in de 1980's."

"So after your grandparents left the prison, they finally escaped to the South, right?"

"It waj not so eajy. Dey had no money so dey borrowed some prom a pormer student. My grandpader pelt so bad, he wrote a promise note so ip dat man needj money, he can get someting from his priend Mr. Kim in Pyongyang."

"That must have been so hard to ask someone for financial help. Did they hire someone like Mr. 3000 to guide them?"

"No, my grandpader went to a church in Yangdong and planned to go prom dere by boat."

I thought about this and imagined that invisible 38th parallel border on the ocean which was so critical for Eunhae's grandparents to cross. I could hear her grandmother's voice again as the story continued.

***

The morning we left Haeju, farmers were bringing their produce to the open market. Women shoppers began their animated bartering for the freshest and best priced vegetables. An invisible force drew me into the action. It had been a month since I had bought groceries and prepared a home-cooked meal for anyone. I had a longing to feed someone and this shopping activity would be a perfect cover from the suspecting eyes of the officials guarding the gate.

"How much for the rice?" and even before he could give the answer, I added, "No, that's too much."

"C'mon, lady, that's the going rate around here these days. It's hard to find rice anywhere now." The farmer really looked injured.

"Okay, just reduce it a little," I insisted. My husband looked away in embarrassment. If only he knew how my bartering skills enabled me to feed our large family and our regular guests. I purchased the rice at a slightly better price.

I proceeded down the row of vendors and carts examining thick leaves of spinach, large green chili peppers, green onions and cucumbers. Soon I amassed a large bundle of vegetables, which I wrapped in my large silk kerchief and carried on my head.

"How can you be thinking of food at this time?" my husband whispered to me.

"Even Diamond Mountain has to be viewed after eating," I replied quoting an old proverb.

"Besides, it makes us look more natural."

As we passed over the peak of Nong-Dang hill we were stunned to see patrolmen checking every passer-by. There was no guard there the day before.

One of the guards stopped my husband.

"May I see your ID, sir?"

"I – I left it at home." My husband responded hesitantly. He was so bad at lying!

"Just wait here." The patrolman shook his head at the overused excuse.

At the same time a woman came carrying a child on her back and a load on her head. She saw the vegetables sticking out of the corners of the bundle on my head and the vegetable-buying itch struck her. She turned to a farmer and began bartering. But a patrolman interrupted her and started questioning her. I was afraid of being caught too and sped away as fast as my tired little legs could carry me.

What happened to my husband? Did they catch him or was he able to get away? I sat down under a pine tree and prayed. Lord, You are a faithful God. You protected us, reunited us and brought us this far. Please help my husband to escape and meet me at the rendezvous point. And Lord, I have the direction sense of a headless chicken. Help me find this place. In Jesus' Name.

Having said this prayer, a curious calm came over me. Perhaps it was because I remembered how God delivered us out of this type of danger so recently.

The sound of footsteps made me turn around hoping to see my husband. Instead, I saw a young man with thick books under one arm.

"Do you know the way to Yong-Dang? Is it this way?" I pointed to the direction I was headed.

"No, ma'am, you'll end up in Haeju if you go that way. Yong-Dang is this direction and I'm going there."

Thank you, Lord, for providing me a guide! We walked together. I tried to walk a bit faster to keep up and then he slowed down to make it easier for me.

"What brings you to Yong-Dang?" he asked. He eyed me with curiosity but with a well-bred gentleness.

"I am going to Yong-Dang Church."

"You are escaping to south aren't you?" he asked in a lower voice.

"I am going to the church there," I said evading his question. "Do you know the name of the minister?"

"His name is Reverend Kim."

"So are you a Christian?" I asked him, since he knew about the church.

"My teachers have told me that there is no god, so I cannot believe in any religion."

It was then that I realized how much education has changed in that short time since the communists came into power. I peered into his eyes. They were such intelligent eyes, reminding me of my own sons. His eyebrows were full and thick and above the left one was a mole. Ah, he must be very smart.

"Is that what you believe?" I asked hoping for an intelligent answer.

"Well, when I read history, I see many evils were done using the power of the churches and Buddhist temples."

"Do you think evil was done before Buddhism or Christianity?"

"Well, yes, it seems any time people have power or wealth, there is greed and they do many evil things. But if everyone shared equally with one another, then there would be no poverty..."

"Do you think there was a time like that?"

"I cannot think of one that worked." He looked down at the rocks on unpaved road as if examining human history on a flat surface.

"I read in the Bible, in the book of Acts when the Christian church just began, they started to live like

that. The people who believed all cared for each other and shared everything together. Even then, it didn't last long either."

"That sounds like the society communism is striving for."

"Do you believe that North Korea can be like that?" I already knew my opinion and looked up at the distant maple trees which burned red and orange.

"I hope so. I was told I may get a scholarship to study in Moscow. They will teach us how they succeeded."

"Do you think the Soviet Union has really succeeded in creating a perfect society where everyone is equal?" I asked trying not to raise my voice.

"You know," he said with a sigh. "I have my doubts. Recently, they had a terrible famine. But do you think that Christians can have an ideal society?" He looked at me, politely hiding his firm belief in the negative.

"No. As long as people are people, there will be problems. Even good and kind people can do or think bad things. That's why they realize they need God. But God alone can love everyone fully and equally even knowing all our faults."

"How do you know this? How can you be sure? Do you have proof?"

"The proof isn't something I can teach like a math formula or an eloquent argument. The proof is Jesus."

"A man?" he asked incredulously.

"He was a man but he was God Who put on human frailty, to teach us how to live and he took away all our punishment for our faults."

"I'm sorry ma'am, but what you say sounds too much like a fable or fairytale. I want real hard evidence." He turned away and looked ahead. "I want a future where science is king and everyone will be educated."

I realized I would never be able to convince him with words. But I liked this young man and wished I could do something for him, like feed him a good meal.

We walked in silence for a bit and he started kicking some of the bigger rocks out of my path.

"The Bible says if you believe in your heart and confess with your mouth that Jesus Christ is Lord then you will be saved," I said breaking the silence as I saw a building that looked like it could be the church.

"Hmm. That saying is familiar. My grandmother used to go to church and she used to quote such phrases."

"Thank you for walking with me." I opened my scarf and took out my two beautiful cucumbers. "Please take these. Cucumbers will give you energy. I'm sorry I don't have anything already cooked to give you."

He hesitated but looked longingly at the cucumbers as he tried to refuse. I was pleased with this show of good manners and quickly put them into his hands.

*"Go in peace and please consider what I've told you,"
I said as we parted ways.*

*"Yes, I will. Thank you very much for a good talk and
for the cucumbers." He bowed politely and went on
his way. Lord, please bless all the things that I said
and remove any unnecessary part. Only bring that
young man out of the darkness of communism and
into the marvelous light of life with You. And please,
Lord, help my husband to escape and find me here. I
entered the church and saw a small round woman
with a kind face. I knew it must be Pastor Kim's wife.*

"Hello, are you Mrs. Kim, the pastor's wife?"

"Yes, are you here looking for someone?"

*"Yes, my husband was here yesterday but he got
stopped by the patrolman."*

*"Don't worry. These things happen all the time. Even
if they catch you seven times, you will be able to pass
through safely with God's help. Don't you worry."
Then she noticed my physical condition and added,
"You really need a good rest. Please go over to that
small house. Our church custodian and his wife live
there. They can get you something to refresh you after
your hard journey."*

*She leaned closer to me and whispered, "Do you see
that lady? She's the custodian's wife. Just follow her
from a distance. Make sure no one from the village
sees you." She smiled and then returned to sweeping
the church floor which struck me as odd since she
was the pastor's wife. I marveled at her humble
servant heart.*

The custodian's wife lived a life of practicing hospitality. She wanted to feed me, but she didn't have much food. So the rice and vegetables I brought were put to good use.

We rolled up our sleeves, side by side over the small coal stove. I steamed the spinach and batter-fried the peppers. She toasted the remaining sesame seeds she had. The seeds smelled a bit rancid but it could not be helped. The strong smell of sesame oil from the seeds induced a bit of nausea but the homey feeling of standing in front of a sizzling and steaming stove perked me up. It felt so good to be doing a familiar activity again.

Cooking was what I did most of the day at home. All seemed well and normal again for a moment. We gave thanks for the nice side dishes we made and we ate the fruit of our labors.

The custodian's wife ate in silence, relishing every minute. It was clear that she hadn't eaten well in a long time. Whatever she did have, she quickly gave away to help others. Now for the first time, she could enjoy a little. She was so engrossed in eating that her silence reminded me of a Korean proverb on eating: "When two are eating, even if one should die, no one would know."

"Excuse me," she said quite suddenly. "I must go out to see if there is anyone else I can help," I wondered if there were some secret signal between her and the minister's wife. They seemed to have an unofficial covert mission to help people get south. I wondered what happened to my husband. So I just closed my eyes and prayed.

I looked up at the sound of approaching footsteps and saw my husband coming into the house guided by the custodian's wife. My husband's face lit up when he saw me. He sat down at the small table on the floor and was happy to start eating the very same rice and vegetables he tried to dissuade me from buying earlier.

"How did you escape?" I asked.

"The guard told me to wait because I didn't have an ID. Then he went to investigate a woman with a big load. She was carrying a child who was screaming loudly. The woman ignored the guard as she was trying to buy some produce. He and another guard found some South Korean currency from her load and were instantly suspicious. Then suddenly a third guard came running and said something in a panic. The senior guard left in a hurry with the messenger and he told the other guard to investigate the woman. While he was so busy interrogating the woman, I ran past the gate and down the hill as fast as I could. I didn't look back. I just ran for my life. They didn't even chase after me."

"Where did you go from there?"

"I was worried for you, since you didn't know the way to Yong-Dang. I looked for you everywhere. But I had to slink around avoiding any guards, who were lurking everywhere. I went into a farmhouse and started to help them chop firewood to look like one of the workers. Then I asked a boy in the house to look for a lost grandma. But he said he couldn't find one. I couldn't wait there forever, so I walked to the church."

"Praise, God."

"Yes, thank God."

The next day was Sunday. We went to Yong-Dang church for the Sunday service and prayed. A group of people who were to board the same boat met and agreed to depart at midnight.

Monday came. We woke from a light sleep when we received the signal for departure. The moon was so bright that it made us uneasy, as we quietly walked down to the shore. There the boat to freedom awaited us. We rolled our pants and skirts up to our knees and safely stepped onto the deck. The small boat quietly glided southward. The calm and quiet sea appeared unusually eerie in the alarming brightness of the moon.

Suddenly, we heard a loud roar of an engine.

"It's a patrol boat! I think it's chasing us!" whispered the boatman in a panic. "Everyone lower your heads as much as possible!"

12 HuiJeong's Prayer

A phone call interrupted Eunhae's story at the most suspenseful moment. She silently mouthed "Sorry" as she answered in Korean. I took that as my cue to leave. But she handed me a plastic wrapped plate full of goodies for Maddie, who thoroughly enjoyed it while I regaled her with what I learned of Eunhae's grandparents' story. I don't know if she was fully satisfied to learn that a panic attack kept Eunhae's grandfather frozen in indecision just waiting at a friend's house. But she did enjoy the part about Eunhae's grandmother demanding her husband's release and the miraculous opportunity to escape due to the holiday.

A few days later, Eunhae appeared at my door, bringing, as it was her custom, something to share. She held a piece of paper in her other hand.

"Risa, I want you to try dis good drink," she said as she lifted the perspiring quart-size canning jar full of cloudy, brown liquid. "Itj cinnamon punch. Itjs reeeaally good in hot summer weader."

"But it's brown."

She laughed and waved her hand in the air as if to wipe away my hesitation. "Lotta drinkj are brown, like tea, cola…"

"But what are those brown blobs on the bottom?"

"Ah, doje are dried persimmonj. Dey add good plabor."

"And what are those white things floating on the top?"

"Oh, you don't know pine nuts? I hear Italian people uje dis lot in cooking."

"Pine nuts. I see," I said as I got two glasses as it looked inevitable that I would have to try some. I wondered why anyone would put nuts in a drink as if to pose a choking hazard.

"Wherej Maddie?" Eunhae asked as she poured from the jar into two glasses not the three she expected.

"She's been gone a lot more lately," I told her. "I do think she and Brian will get back together." I noted a sweet smile on Eunhae as I raised my glass to my mouth to take the tiniest sip. I used my teeth as a filter to only get the liquid.

An intensely powerful cinnamon and ginger sweetness woke up every taste bud in my mouth.

"Wow! That's some drink!" I managed to say as I caught a few pine nuts and started to chew. The nutty flavor, mixed with the cinnamon and ginger, added a mellow finish. "No alcohol, right?" I asked wondering about the burn.

Eunhae laughed. "No, just cinnamon, ginger and sugar and you can eat de sopt persimmon apter. Like dejert plus drink."

Eunhae's face suddenly turned serious and she said, "Risa, I habe pabor to ask you."

"Sure, what is it?"

"Can you help me pronounce deje wordj?" she said as she showed me a list of hand scrawled words. "Regal wordj."

"Legal words," I corrected. I read aloud, "No-fault, plaintiff, subpoena…"

"Dat one ij soobpohna."

"No, suhPEEna is how we say subpoena."

"What kind of word ij dat?"

"It's from Latin. Sub means under and poena means penalty. English simplified the pronunciation of the OE and made it just an EE sound. It means you could be punished if you don't do as it orders."

"Oh. Prom Latin?" Eunhae cocked her head to one side thinking about this. "Hmm. Like Korean haj lotj of wordj prom old Chineje but we pronounce bery dipprently." She pointed with her index finger to the next word on the paper, "How about dis one, waiber."

"Waiver," I corrected. "Make sure your upper teeth are on your lower lip and use your vocal cords to make the V sound."

"WayVVVeh"

"Close enough," I said not venturing to emphasize the "er" sound. "Now what is this word? Iletre- I can't quite read it."

"Ileturebabble breakdown," Eunhae read. "I understand breakdown but don't know what de pirst one sayj."

"You sure it's an 'L' sound?"

Eunhae tapped her forehead and cried out, "Oh, datj not 'l' itj 'r.' I just wrote like it soundj to me."

"So it says irre...oh, irretrievable."

"Illetureebabul."

"No, try it from the back first," I suggested covering the first part of the word and moving my finger to the left syllable by syllable. "Like this: ble, then able, then trievable, then retrievable and finally, irretrievable!"

Eunhae mouthed the syllables silently watching my finger. "Ilretribable!" she cried triumphantly.

"Close enough."

"Whatj meaning?"

"It means you can't get it back."

The spark in her eyes disappeared and she looked away. "Um. I was wondering about the boat escape." I thought it would be good to change the subject. "Did the patrol boat stop them?"

"No. De patrol boat passed dem. Dey were sape. Den dey had to go to the repugee shelter in Kaesong."

"Where is Kaesong?"

"Well, it ij bery close to de border between Nort and Sout Korea. Now it ij in Nort Korea but bepore de Korean War it waj part ob Sout Korea. So dey could take train to Pusan prom dere."

"All this time, the children had no idea where their parents were. What's the name of the oldest child again?"

"HuiJeong. The Hui part meanj 'joy.' All de sisterj have Jeong as de middle name."

"Heejong." I mimicked.

Eunhae blinked a couple of times in surprise and then said, "Close enoup." And we both burst out laughing.

"So what did the children do while waiting for their parents to come?"

"Well," Eunhae began. "It must habe been so hard por my moder taking care ob all her broderj and sisterj, especially her sick sister."

Then I imagined what it would be like to be bedridden for

two months counting the days waiting for her parents to return. What was it like to be in physical pain, with a mind full of worry and a heart full of guilt, unable to comfort her anxious siblings?

***

"It's been five weeks and five days," I rehearsed aloud in a hoarse whisper. "Or is it six days?"

"What did you say, Big Sister?" My sister peered over me, her worried expression like a lonely, full moon. She swapped out the fever-warmed washcloth with a fresh cool one on my forehead.

In the sparse room where I was quarantined from the rest of the family, there was only this heavy quilt that I was lying on. These quilt-mattresses were rolled up and put away during the day in the other rooms. Only mine stayed on the coal-heated floor day after day, night after night. On the small table sat a picture of my mother and me as a baby. Being the firstborn, there were more formal pictures of me than my younger siblings. A chamber pot hid in the corner. Other than these, there were no companions, just my next younger sister.

"I'm so sorry to be a --" I tried to say as a violent series of coughs seized my throat.

"Don't try to talk, Big Sister," SookJeong held my hand and it was then she found in my enclosed fist, the blood-stained handkerchief I didn't want her to find. The disease was progressing fast.

Worry creased lines on her forehead but she said nothing. She rummaged through the built-in wall cupboards where the linens are kept and found more handkerchiefs and handed me one.

Dejectedly, she left the room with the chamber pot. Who would imagine my fiercest rival would become my most tender nurse. I'm so sorry, my sister. I should be the one out there cooking and taking care of our younger siblings. Lord, why?

My younger sister was so strong, so wild, and so smart. People would always compliment me on my looks and say nothing to her. But sister, you really are beautiful. But she was always the star pupil in every class. I inadvertently helped her because my study habits involved shouting my lessons at the top of my lungs.

"HuiJeong, can you study a little quieter?" Father would say.

"No, Father," I'd reply. "I need to say it loud so it can stay in my brain."

"Well, alright." Father conceded since studying was so important.

But my younger sister listened and memorized every word and learned everything two grades ahead of her classmates.

She was a wild tomboy who was curious about everything. She had a crazy sense of humor, too. Once, during morning exercises, as Father made all his children get up early daily and do calisthenics, SookJeong crossed her eyes while doing jumping jacks. Father nearly had a heart attack!

Those long-ago days seemed so precious to me now. We had moved to a place we don't know and worst of all, we don't know what became of our parents.

Sometimes, my younger siblings poked their heads into my room. I pretended to be asleep. I couldn't talk with them as I knew the coughing would start. Then the blood. That would scare them.

Lord, is it time for me to go? If you take me, give them another daughter to fill the empty space in my mother's heart.

The fortune teller told my mother that I was the healthiest baby he had ever seen and that I would live a really long life. Why did my strong Christian mother see a fortune teller? Seems she kept some pagan souvenirs even as she embraced Christian faith. Is there any worshipper who is completely untainted by human superstition? Superstitions give us a false sense of control over the unknowable even if it's completely untrue.

Another day slipped into evening and I fell in and out of consciousness with what felt like an elephant sitting on my chest. Each breath was labor. But as long as I had breath, I could still pray.

> *God our Healer, restore my health*
> *Our life in You is our great wealth*
> *But length of life You alone know*
> *Let me see them before I go.*
>
> *God our Provider, see our need.*
> *Bring our parents home safe with speed*

Why they tarry so very slow?
Let me see them before I go

God our Father, adopt us now
With humble thanks before You bow
Though orphaned, Heaven's hope will glow
Let me see them before I go.

The dining hour started and with it the clanging of
steel bowls and the clicking of silver chopsticks and
adult voices teaching children dining manners. Then
there was a creak. I trained my yearning ear to listen
for the exact pitch of the worn, wooden gate since I
came here. I hoped for this sound for over a month. I
must ... I must rise to see out the window. Dizziness
overwhelmed me but I had to see. Did I really see
them? Or is it my imagination?

"Mother! Father!" I shouted with all my might.
Feet hurried to the room.

"Sister!" SookJeong cried. "Wha- What are you
doing?" Then the stampede of other feet followed and
they were all startled at my rising and clinging to the
window. I managed to point. Outside my mother's
feet moved faster and faster to the door. Tears
flooded on all our faces. At last, we were reunited.

***

"So did HuiJeong get better?"

"She did for a bit after my grandparentj arribed home. But
in de supring time she died."

"That must have been so hard on your grandmother."

"Yes. But de hardest ting por her waj dat she could not gibe HuiJeong a proper burial."

"Why not?"

"You know each pamily has deir own burial ground like small hill. And my grandpaderj ancesterj are all buried dere. But daughters get buried in deir hujband's pamily burial plot. HuiJeong waj considered already grown woman and single."

Before I could find a way to politely express my outrage, Eunhae's cellphone rang and this time she looked nervous. I wanted to ask her why she wanted to learn to say those "regal" words. But she quickly headed to the door saying, "Sorry I habe to take dis." And she waved goodbye.

In that brief time, we shared frustration, laughter, tears and now, indignation for the aunt she never knew. But I had no idea that it would be the last time I would see her.

13 Moving Day

My old friends, Peace and Quiet, returned to the house after Maddie moved back with her husband. Maddie called occasionally and recounted the ways they were re-discovering each other and learning how to build some daily shared experiences.

With fewer work hours during the summer months, I could actually read more than a few sentences at a time without interruptions. I reached the part of my mystery novel, where the villain just set off a bomb when I was jolted by a loud hiss-moan-squeal of an air brake. I got up to peer through the peephole. A large moving truck parked itself in front of Eunhae's house.

A slender, young Asian woman with reddish-colored hair walked around the large truck. She carried a large cardboard box that she could barely see over. She walked towards my house. Before she could ease her shoulder into the doorbell, I opened the door. Surprised, she took a step back and then quickly recovered herself.

"Hi, I'm Jenna, Eunhae's daughter. Are you Lisa?"

"Yes," I replied happy to know that Eunhae mentioned me to her daughter. "Good to meet you. Sorry to startle you. I got up to see what the noise was about. Did something happen to … your mom? I hadn't seen her for several weeks."

"Not to her. Her sister in Korea is having surgery," Jenna explained as she lowered the box on my porch. "So my mom figured she would move to Korea and live there and just visit me occasionally. I'm moving her things into storage. She asked me to give you and Maddie a few things."

"She moved all the way to Korea just to help?" I asked, unable to disguise my incredulity.

"Oh, yes, hospitals in Korea are not like the hospitals here."

"I thought South Korea has great health care," I stated wishing to argue the case for not moving.

"Yes, they have very good, reasonable health care since taxes cover most expenses. And medicine is really cheap. But they don't give the same services. When someone goes to the hospital, a family member or friend has to come and help. They don't provide meals or help with anything not related to the medical treatment. So a family member does many of the things that nurses and medical staff do here. My aunt is single and her friends are all working so my mom went to help her."

"Oh," I said trying to put this new piece of information into perspective. "So that's how they can offer such reasonable healthcare. But won't your mom come back after your aunt has recovered?"

At this, Jenna smiled sadly and gave a big sigh. "You know, she only moved here to be closer to my father."

"Father?" I asked with more surprise than I intended and tried to cover my faux pas. "I'm sorry, I didn't know your father was alive."

Jenna laughed that same congenial laugh that Eunhae had. It reassured me that I didn't offend her. I observed her face and could see only a vague resemblance to Eunhae in her eyes. Her face was rather long and angular and so she didn't remind me of Eunhae at all.

"Oh, she didn't tell you?...Right, she hardly ever shares about herself or her problems."

"Please come in," I said remembering my manners and helped Jenna bring in her box. "Could I get you something to drink?"

"Oh, no, thanks. I can't stay long. I have to give the movers instructions and arrange for the cleaning people to come."

"Your mom is very neat," I reassured her. "I don't think you'd need to clean up much."

"She's neat," she agreed. "But I need to have someone professionally make sure the kimchi smells are gone for the next renters." At this, she covered her mouth and giggled into her hand. Then she pointed to the jars in the box. "Please remember to cover these jars in two zippered plastic bags so your refrigerator doesn't smell."

"Oh, don't worry," I said imagining how quickly Maddie would be over to relieve me of the jars.

"But please, continue," I urged her. "What didn't your mom tell me?"

"You see my parents have been separated for about ten years. I had just started college then. I never understood why because they seemed to get along. My best explanation is that my dad went through some kind of midlife crisis and wanted a different life. He wasn't in touch with me much either. All of my mom's friends and family told her to move on. But she wouldn't. She just kept waiting."

"Waiting for what?"

"She kept hoping that they would get back together. But last month, the divorce papers came and she finally decided to let him go."

"I didn't know. I guess I never even asked her if she were married." Then I remembered words like "irretrievable breakdown" that she asked how to pronounce.

"That sounds like her," Jenna smiled, looking away as if imagining her mother. "She would much rather help someone else with their problems than speak about her own. Plus, she loves feeding people."

"Yes, I know this well." I smiled knowingly and Jenna picked up on this.

"Oh dear, I hope you weren't forced into…" Jenna interjected with some alarm.

"No," I assured her. "In fact, your mom helped me overcome a lot of fear about trying new foods. So I'm grateful to her."

"And I'm thankful for you!" Jenna's eyes glistened. "You probably didn't know but when she went around the neighborhood introducing herself, you were the only ones who received her warmly and befriended her. I was so worried when she left her comfortable neighborhood where she had lots of friends. But when she met you, she felt more at home. So thank you." She leaned her head toward my shoulder and gave me a side hug which I reciprocated awkwardly as I was not used to hugs from people I had just met.

"Anyway, she said she is very sorry she could not come in person to say goodbye. Here are some tokens she wanted you to have."

I recognized the light gray green plate that had the mochi that she brought over the first time we met.

"It was her favorite dish because it is made to look like the traditional Korean celadon ceramic pottery. The fact that she wants you to have it means she really likes you."

Who brings a stranger a favorite dish? I guess risks are taken in relationships. Eunhae was willing to take risks.

"Well, your Mom not only fed us but she also taught us a lot by sharing stories about her grandmother."

"Oh, that!" Jenna gave a quick swipe with her hand in embarrassment. I recognized her gestures and facial expressions. They were so much like Eunhae's. So while Jenna didn't inherit Eunhae's looks or her speech patterns, she definitely inherited her non-verbal language. "I hope you and Maddie didn't get bored with all those stories."

"Oh, no! We enjoyed them very much." I couldn't help but smile when I thought about how things turned around for Maddie. "In fact, I think those stories helped us put our modern day troubles into perspective."

"Yeah," Jenna sighed. "When I was a kid, I didn't appreciate those stories much. It made my problems seem so small. Kids would tease me at school and then I get a story about how people get killed for believing in God. Or, I'd have trouble with my homework and I would get a story about how my grandmother skipped two grades after escaping North Korea. Nothing compared to the hardships my grandmother and great-grandparents had. Yet, they survived and lived to thank God."

"I really admire your great-grandmother's faith. I found it inspiring."

"Thanks. I'm sure it encouraged my mom that you listened. Perhaps, sharing those stories was a way for her to reach into her roots and make it easier to let go of her broken dreams here."

"I'm so sorry that I couldn't have helped her in some way," I manage to say while reprimanding myself for not asking Eunhae more personal questions.

"You actually did help her," Jenna said firmly reaching for both my hands. She gave my hands a squeeze. "You listened." I could see tears well up again and she quickly turned towards the door. "Thanks, again, Lisa. And please thank Maddie, too. I have to go." With that, she hurried out the door.

"Thank your Mom and tell her to write!" I called after her. She turned around and called back, "Don't worry. She has your address. I'm sure she'll write!"

A month later, on another quiet day, the doorbell rang. The peephole revealed a lovely, tanned face framed in a hijab. She was holding a plate full of oval-shaped meatballs. Here we go again...

Internet Resources for Korean Cooking

If you are interested in learning more about Korean cooking, I recommend the following websites:

www.maangchi.com
www.koreanbapsang.com
www.aeriskitchen.com

These internet chefs not only introduce you to Korean foods with detailed recipes but also show you how to recreate the dishes with entertaining videos.

I prefer a milder kimchi so below are my favorite recipes.

For a Napa cabbage kimchi:
http://gryffonridge.com/mild-kimchi-with-pear-apple/

For a pickled cucumber kimchi:
http://www.eatingwell.com/recipe/250130/quick-cucumber-kimchi/

For a radish (daikon) kimchi:
https://www.maangchi.com/recipe/kkakdugi

I have made all these without fish sauce and it tastes fine.

Crossing Barriers

ABOUT THE AUTHOR

Helen Hahn-Steichen teaches English as a Second Language. She immigrated to the U.S. as a child and grew up in Hawaii and worked in high tech. Throughout her life, she was privileged to meet people from many different countries and enjoyed learning about their cultures.

77708241R00075

Made in the USA
San Bernardino, CA
27 May 2018